If you are a supervisor-in-training or teaching a supervision course, you must read this book. These authors are expert supervisors/teachers/researchers who know what they are talking about. They offer empirically supported ideas for how to supervise. The book is readable and authoritative and an important next step in this rapidly emerging field.
—**Clara E. Hill, PhD**, Department of Psychology, University of Maryland, College Park

The authors draw from their previous seminal contributions to the supervision literature to offer a pragmatic and wise road map for conducting psychotherapy supervision. As clearly described in this highly engaging volume, critical events make up the "stuff" of supervision. Ladany, Friedlander, and Nelson help us to capture these critical events and navigate through them successfully. They offer an appealing balance of model development and clinical examples that will be welcomed by novice and experienced supervisors alike.
—**Janine M. Bernard, PhD,** Professor Emeritus of Counseling and Counselor Education, Syracuse University; Legacy Award Recipient of the Association for Counselor Education and Supervision; coauthor of *Fundamentals of Clinical Supervision*

Ladany, Friedlander, and Nelson have provided a resource that supervisors of clinical work will find resonates with their challenges in practice. Four critical events of supervision are the foundation of the book and provide powerful reminders of the complexity of the supervisory process. The authors' conceptualization and untangling of role conflict, skill deficits, parallel processes, and cultural sensitivities in supervision is based on years of empirical work and practice wisdom. Practitioners can turn to this book when on the horns of a dilemma to find a carefully articulated approach toward resolution.
—**Elizabeth L. Holloway, PhD ABPP,** Graduate School of Leadership and Change, Antioch University, Yellow Springs, OH

This book provides a highly useful and accessible model for effective supervision, supported by empirical research and the authors' extensive clinical experience. Using case examples and transcripts to illustrate common challenging situations, the authors provide clear and practical guidance for actual supervision practice. I highly recommend this book for both supervisors and supervisors-in-training.
—**Tony Rousmaniere, PsyD,** Clinical Faculty, University of Washington, Seattle

Supervision Essentials for

# the Critical Events in Psychotherapy Supervision Model

# Clinical Supervision
# Essentials Series

# CLINICAL SUPERVISION ESSENTIALS

HANNA LEVENSON *and* ARPANA G. INMAN, Series Editors

Supervision Essentials for

# the Critical Events in Psychotherapy Supervision Model

Nicholas Ladany, Myrna L. Friedlander,
and Mary Lee Nelson

**American Psychological Association • Washington, DC**

Published by
American Psychological Association
750 First Street, NE
Washington, DC 20002
www.apa.org

To order
APA Order Department
P.O. Box 92984
Washington, DC 20090-2984
Tel: (800) 374-2721; Direct: (202) 336-5510
Fax: (202) 336-5502; TDD/TTY: (202) 336-6123
Online: www.apa.org/pubs/books
E-mail: order@apa.org

In the U.K., Europe, Africa, and the Middle East, copies may be ordered from
American Psychological Association
3 Henrietta Street
Covent Garden, London
WC2E 8LU England

Typeset in Minion by Circle Graphics, Inc., Columbia, MD

Printer: United Book Press, Inc., Baltimore, MD
Cover Designer: Mercury Publishing Services, Inc., Rockville, MD

The opinions and statements published are the responsibility of the authors, and such opinions and statements do not necessarily represent the policies of the American Psychological Association.

Library of Congress Cataloging-in-Publication Data

Names: Ladany, Nicholas, author. | Friedlander, Myrna L., author. | Nelson, Mary Lee, author.
Title: Supervision essentials for the critical events in psychotherapy supervision model / Nicholas Ladany, Myrna L. Friedlander, and Mary Lee Nelson.
Description: Washington, DC : American Psychological Association, [2016] | Includes bibliographical references and index.
Identifiers: LCCN 2015050631 | ISBN 9781433822513 | ISBN 1433822512
Subjects: LCSH: Psychotherapists—Supervision of. | Psychotherapy—Study and teaching. | Psychotherapists—Training of.
Classification: LCC RC459 .L335 2016 | DDC 616.89/14—dc23 LC record available at http://lccn.loc.gov/2015050631

British Library Cataloguing-in-Publication Data
A CIP record is available from the British Library.

Printed in the United States of America
First Edition

http://dx.doi.org/10.1037/14916-000

To our families
Randa, Nisrine, Mona, and Farah
Lou and Lee
Randy and Eric

# Contents

# Foreword to the Clinical Supervision Essentials Series

We are both clinical supervisors. We teach courses on supervision of students who are in training to become therapists. We give workshops on supervision and consult with supervisors about their supervision practices. We write and do research on the topic. To say we eat and breathe supervision might be a little exaggerated, but only slightly. We are fully invested in the field and in helping supervisors provide the most informed and helpful guidance to those learning the profession. We also are committed to helping supervisees/consultees/trainees become better collaborators in the supervisory endeavor by understanding their responsibilities in the supervisory process.

What is supervision? Supervision is critical to the practice of therapy. As stated by Edward Watkins[1] in the *Handbook of Psychotherapy Supervision*, "Without the enterprise of psychotherapy supervision, . . . the practice of psychotherapy would become highly suspect and would or should cease to exist" (p. 603).

Supervision has been defined as

> an intervention provided by a more senior member of a profession to a more junior colleague or colleagues who typically (but not always) are members of that same profession. This relationship
>
> - is evaluative and hierarchical,
> - extends over time, and

---

[1] Watkins, C. E., Jr. (Ed.). (1997). *Handbook of psychotherapy supervision*. New York, NY: Wiley.

■ has the simultaneous purposes of enhancing the professional functioning of the more junior person(s); monitoring the quality of professional services offered to the clients that she, he, or they see; and serving as a gatekeeper for the particular profession the supervisee seeks to enter. (p. 9)[2]

It is now widely acknowledged in the literature that supervision is a "distinct activity" in its own right.[3] One cannot assume that being an excellent therapist generalizes to being an outstanding supervisor. Nor can one imagine that good supervisors can just be "instructed" in how to supervise through purely academic, didactic means.

So how does one become a good supervisor?

Supervision is now recognized as a core competency domain for psychologists[4,5] and other mental health professionals. Guidelines have been created to facilitate the provision of competent supervision across professional groups and internationally (e.g., American Psychological Association,[6] American Association of Marriage and Family Therapy,[7] British Psychological Society,[8,9] Canadian Psychological Association[10]).

[2] Bernard, J. M., & Goodyear, R. K. (2014). *Fundamentals of clinical supervision* (5th ed.). Boston, MA: Pearson.

[3] Bernard, J. M., & Goodyear, R. K. (2014). *Fundamentals of clinical supervision* (5th ed.). Boston, MA: Pearson.

[4] Fouad, N., Grus, C. L., Hatcher, R. L., Kaslow, N. J., Hutchings, P. S., Madson, M. B., . . . Crossman, R. E. (2009). Competency benchmarks: A model for understanding and measuring competence in professional psychology across training levels. *Training and Education in Professional Psychology, 3* (4 Suppl.), S5–S26. http://dx.doi.org/10.1037/a0015832

[5] Kaslow, N. J., Rubin, N. J., Bebeau, M. J., Leigh, I. W., Lichtenberg, J. W., Nelson, P. D., . . . Smith, I. L. (2007). Guiding principles and recommendations for the assessment of competence. *Professional Psychology: Research and Practice, 38*, 441–51. http://dx.doi.org/10.1037/0735-7028.38.5.441

[6] American Psychological Association. (2014). *Guidelines for clinical supervision in health service psychology.* Retrieved from http://www.apa.org/about/policy/guidelines-supervision.pdf

[7] American Association of Marriage and Family Therapy. (2007). *AAMFT approved supervisor designation standards and responsibilities handbook.* Retrieved from http://www.aamft.org/imis15/Documents/Approved_Supervisor_handbook.pdf

[8] British Psychological Society. (2003). *Policy guidelines on supervision in the practice of clinical psychology.* Retrieved from http://www.conatus.co.uk/assets/uploaded/downloads/policy_and_guidelines_on_supervision.pdf

[9] British Psychological Society. (2010). *Professional supervision: Guidelines for practice for educational psychologists.* Retrieved from http://www.ucl.ac.uk/educational-psychology/resources/DECP%20Supervision%20report%20Nov%202010.pdf

[10] Canadian Psychological Association. (2009). *Ethical guidelines for supervision in psychology: Teaching, research, practice and administration.* Retrieved from http://www.cpa.ca/docs/File/Ethics/EthicalGuidelinesSupervisionPsychologyMar2012.pdf

The *Guidelines for Clinical Supervision in Health Service Psychology*[11] are built on several assumptions, specifically that supervision

- requires formal education and training;
- prioritizes the care of the client/patient and the protection of the public;
- focuses on the acquisition of competence by and the professional development of the supervisee;
- requires supervisor competence in the foundational and functional competency domains being supervised;
- is anchored in the current evidence base related to supervision and the competencies being supervised;
- occurs within a respectful and collaborative supervisory relationship that includes facilitative and evaluative components and is established, maintained, and repaired as necessary;
- entails responsibilities on the part of the supervisor and supervisee;
- intentionally infuses and integrates the dimensions of diversity in all aspects of professional practice;
- is influenced by both professional and personal factors, including values, attitudes, beliefs, and interpersonal biases;
- is conducted in adherence to ethical and legal standards;
- uses a developmental and strength-based approach;
- requires reflective practice and self-assessment by the supervisor and supervisee;
- incorporates bidirectional feedback between the supervisor and supervisee;
- includes evaluation of the acquisition of expected competencies by the supervisee;
- serves a gatekeeping function for the profession; and
- is distinct from consultation, personal psychotherapy, and mentoring.

The importance of supervision can be attested to by the increase in state laws and regulations that certify supervisors and the required multiple supervisory practica and internships that graduate students in all professional programs must complete. Furthermore, research has

---

[11] American Psychological Association. (2014). *Guidelines for clinical supervision in health service psychology.* Retrieved from http://www.apa.org/about/policy/guidelines-supervision.pdf

confirmed[12] the high prevalence of supervisory responsibilities among practitioners—specifically that between 85% and 90% of all therapists eventually become clinical supervisors within the first 15 years of practice.

So now we see the critical importance of good supervision and its high prevalence. We also have guidelines for its competent practice and an impressive list of objectives. But is this enough to become a good supervisor? Not quite. One of the best ways to learn is from highly regarded supervisors—the experts in the field—those who have the procedural knowledge[13] to know what to do, when, and why.

Which leads us to our motivation for creating this series. As we looked around for materials that would help us supervise, teach, and research clinical supervision, we were struck by the lack of a coordinated effort to present the essential models of supervision in both a didactic and experiential form through the lens of expert supervisors. What seemed to be needed was a forum where the experts in the field—those with the knowledge *and* the practice—present the basics of their approaches in a readable, accessible, concise fashion and demonstrate what they do in a real supervisory session. The need, in essence, was for a showcase of best practices.

This series, then, is an attempt to do just that. We considered the major approaches to supervisory practice—those that are based on theoretical orientation and those that are metatheoretical. We surveyed psychologists, teachers, clinical supervisors, and researchers domestically and internationally working in the area of supervision. We asked them to identify specific models to include and who they would consider to be experts in this area. We also asked this community of colleagues to identify key issues that typically need to be addressed in supervision sessions. Through this consensus building, we came up with a dream team of 11 supervision experts who not only have developed a working model of supervision but also have been in the trenches as clinical supervisors for years.

---

[12] Rønnestad, M. H., Orlinsky, D. E., Parks, B. K., & Davis, J. D. (1997). Supervisors of psychotherapy: Mapping experience level and supervisory confidence. *European Psychologist, 2,* 191–201.

[13] Schön, D. A. (1987). *Educating the reflective practitioner: Toward a new design for teaching and learning in the professions.* San Francisco, CA: Jossey-Bass.

We asked each expert to write a concise book elucidating her or his approach to supervision. This included highlighting the essential dimensions/key principles, methods/techniques, and structure/process involved, the research evidence for the model, and how common supervisory issues are handled. Furthermore, we asked each author to elucidate the supervisory process by devoting a chapter describing a supervisory session in detail, including transcripts of real sessions, so that the readers could see how the model comes to life in the reality of the supervisory encounter.

In addition to these books, each expert filmed an actual supervisory session with a supervisee so that her or his approach could be demonstrated in practice. APA Books has produced these videos as a series and they are available as DVDs (http://www.apa.org/pubs/videos). Each of these books and videos can be used together or independently, as part of the series or alone, for the reader aspiring to learn how to supervise, for supervisors wishing to deepen their knowledge, for trainees wanting to be better supervisees, for teachers of courses on supervision, and for researchers investigating this pedagogical process.

## ABOUT THIS BOOK

In this book, *Supervision Essentials for the Critical Events in Psychotherapy Supervision Model*, Ladany, Friedlander, and Nelson describe a practice-based, process-oriented approach that is theoretically and empirically informed; their goal is to flesh out what it means to be a responsive supervisor in dealing effectively with the complexity of the supervisory encounter. Using a pantheoretical model founded within a sound supervisory relationship, the reader is taken through a series of steps designed to help the clinical supervisor (and supervisee) handle (and hopefully resolve) several common, but challenging, supervisory dilemmas—such as how to address role conflict and ambiguity, how to handle trainees with deficits, how to work with parallel process, and how to be sensitive to multicultural issues. The key principles and techniques of this "task analytic approach" are vividly conveyed through a multitude of supervisory examples. Reading this book is like having these experienced supervisors, sophisticated researchers, and superb teachers whispering in your ear regarding what strategies are most effective at critical choice points ("critical events") in the supervision work. This is a must-read for those, regardless of orientation or discipline, who want to enhance their capacity for using facilitative moment-to-moment interactions within the supervisory hour.

We thank you for your interest and hope the books in this series enhance your work in a stimulating and relevant way.

Hanna Levenson and Arpana G. Inman

Supervision Essentials for

# the Critical
Events in
Psychotherapy
Supervision
Model

# Introduction

The critical events in psychotherapy supervision model (Ladany, Friedlander, & Nelson, 2005), also known as critical events in supervision, is intended for supervisors and supervisors in training of mental health practitioners. In this book, we focus on the essentials of our model with the intent of providing a general introduction to our approach as well as clinical applications of particular dilemmas. These dilemmas include handling role conflict and ambiguity, addressing skill difficulties and deficits, working through parallel processes, and heightening multicultural awareness. Interested readers can find discussions of several other critical events (e.g., managing countertransference, resolving gender-related misunderstandings, addressing problematic attitudes and behavior) in Ladany et al. (2005).

Our practice-based approach is theoretically and empirically informed. The critical events are applicable across theoretical approaches;

http://dx.doi.org/10.1037/14916-001
*Supervision Essentials for the Critical Events in Psychotherapy Supervision Model*, by N. Ladany, M. L. Friedlander, and M. L. Nelson

however, the bases of the interpersonal aspects of our approach are reflective of interpersonal, contemporary psychoanalytic, and humanistic approaches to supervision (Bromberg, 1982; Friedlander, 2012, 2015; Gill, 2001; Greenberg, 1983; Sarnat, 2016; Skovholt & Ronnestad, 1992). We assume that the client, supervisee, and supervisor are all active participants in the understanding of supervision and therapy processes. Our supervision empirical and theoretical work, along with the work of others, also influenced our selection of dilemmas or critical events.

## OVERVIEW OF THE BOOK

The first chapter introduces the task-analytic paradigm on which the model is based. In it, we define the key principles of our model (e.g., define the relationship using the supervisory working alliance model), the methods and techniques (e.g., interventions and purposeful interactions that the supervisor may use to engage the supervisee), and the structure and processes of supervision, all of which are illustrated with case examples throughout the rest of the book. These case examples provide ways to handle common supervisory issues, such as addressing supervisee competency concerns, conflicts, and multicultural concepts in supervision, as well as the interplay among and between these issues.

Although supervision entails accomplishing numerous tasks, we target specific events or episodes in which there is a critical task to be worked through. In Ladany et al. (2005) and in subsequent writings on the critical events model, we identified 10 critical events that include (a) remediating skill difficulties and deficits, (b) heightening multicultural awareness, (c) negotiating role conflicts, (d) working through countertransference, (e) managing sexual attraction, (f) repairing gender-related misunderstandings, and (g) addressing supervisees' problematic attitudes and behaviors. In Chapters 2, 3, and 4, we focus on four critical events: working through role conflicts (Chapter 2), addressing skill deficits and competency concerns (Chapter 3), and working through parallel process and heightening multicultural awareness (Chapter 4). In addition, Chapter 4 illustrates the manner in which two events can overlap.

Chapter 5 offers additional thoughts on our model. In particular, we consider how the critical events model can be used to train supervisors and consider elements of effective and ineffective supervision that go beyond the model. Moreover, we provide a section on research of the model and how the model can be researched in the future. Chapter 5 also includes close analysis of Nicholas Ladany's videotaped supervisory session with a clinical trainee.[1] The book also includes a list of suggested readings, along with information about how these readings can serve the reader interested in additional aspects of our model.

## PERSONAL JOURNEYS

To further provide context to our supervision model, we offer a summary of our personal journeys to becoming a supervisor. For us, becoming an expert supervisor is a professional lifelong endeavor that is aspirational rather than achievable.

*Nicholas Ladany*: Dr. Ladany has had the good fortune to have written about his road to becoming a professional supervision scholar, educator, and practitioner (Ladany, 2004, 2010). Reflecting back, there seem to be three general themes that can characterize his emergence specifically as the supervision practitioner. The first theme is learning how to do by reading and studying. He never had a supervision course. However, as a doctoral student he was able to study with two faculty whose areas of work were in supervision: Michael Ellis and Micki Friedlander. Having the opportunity to work with two top supervision scholars was without a doubt an extraordinary learning opportunity. In fact, his work in supervision research preceded his actual experiences as a clinician. By reviewing supervision theory and research, and then through having faculty mentors who encouraged his participation in supervision scholarship, he was able to develop at least a theoretical and empirical understanding of the supervision enterprise. In particular, he learned how to look critically

---

[1] *Critical Events in Psychotherapy Supervision* DVD is available from APA at http://www.apa.org/pubs/videos/4310956.aspx.

at the supervision literature and tease out findings that were practically relevant from those that were more likely to be anecdotal.

The second theme to Dr. Ladany's road to becoming a supervision practitioner is learning what not to do from incompetent and abusive supervisors. As he has learned over time, he is not alone in experiencing poor to harmful supervisory experiences (e.g., racist, sexist, homophobic, narcissistic, and/or psychopathological supervisors). What at first he thought was his personal jadedness has led him to believe that his experiences may reflect a larger reality. In other words, as he has talked about and studied supervision, he has come to learn that many supervisees experience poor to harmful supervision. In fact, he has estimated that about a third of the time supervisors are effective, a third of the time they are benign, and a third of the time they are incompetent—perhaps a sad state of affairs for the field, but he also thinks that this reflects what is true of most professions (physicians, lawyers, plumbers). The difficulty is that for supervisors and therapists, psychological harm can be the result of poor performance.

Alternatively, learning what to do from watching highly effective supervisors is a third theme to his road to becoming a supervision practitioner. This learning approach comes from two sources. The first is personally experiencing expert supervisors from the perspective of a supervisee. As mentioned earlier, Mike Ellis and Micki Friedlander were academic mentors of Dr. Ladany in relation to supervision research. They were also expert supervisors for him as he learned the craft and science of therapy. The common elements of both, along with only a few others, involved the development of a strong alliance along with an interpersonal approach to therapist growth. In a similar manner, when training supervisors, Dr. Ladany has witnessed similar things in those that are most effective. In essence, the alliance and an interpersonal approach serve as the foundation upon which supervisee growth occurs.

In sum, the three broad themes or experiences have led Dr. Ladany to be the supervision practitioner he is today and ultimately informed the development of the authors' critical events in supervision model. Dr. Ladany believes true expertise is more an aspiration than an end result. As such, his hope is that he continue to work toward being an effective supervisor as much of the time as possible.

*Micki Friedlander*: Dr. Friedlander's first exposure to supervision was a 1979 seminar on supervision theory during her doctoral studies. Reflecting the profession at that time, the seminar focused primarily on what supervisors do, with little attention to how supervisees respond or how the supervisory relationship is developed. As a teaching assistant the following semester, Dr. Friedlander supervised a group of four students who were actually in her doctoral cohort but not as experienced clinically as she was. This was the most difficult supervision experience of her 35-year (and counting!) career because the dual roles of the students and Dr. Friedlander and her lack of expert status interfered greatly with what she hoped to accomplish with the students. With one supervisee in particular, she had a firsthand experience of a role conflict event, but she was not to fully understand what was going on between the two of them until much later.

At the time Dr. Friedlander was enthralled with psychoanalytic psychotherapy, and although she had read about "parallel process," it seemed quite mystifying. Her "sup of sup" supervisor, Harold Pepinsky, who was light years ahead of his time in scholarship as well as training, told Dr. Friedlander at the end of this summer practicum that he saw his role not only as helping her learn to supervise but also containing her anxiety about doing so. This was an eye opener! The mirroring of supervision and therapy processes has never failed to amaze Dr. Friedlander.

Her "journey" since that first supervision experience reflects an integration of practice with research. Early in her academic career, she became fascinated with the relational aspects of supervision. Viewing supervision as an influence process similar to Strong and Matross's (1973) model of psychotherapy as interpersonal persuasion, Dr. Friedlander studied supervisors' evaluations of trainees whose self-presentations were either defensive or counterdefensive about their clients' progress (Ward, Friedlander, Schoen, & Klein, 1985), the results of which reflected her experience as a trainee and a supervisor. That is, supervision is a catch-22—supervisors tend to view trainees who expose their weaknesses as more socially skilled but evaluate trainees who describe their successes with clients as more self-confident.

Although informative, Dr. Friedlander's early research did little to illuminate how supervisors use the process of supervision to facilitate supervisees' clinical skill development. Consequently, she set out to discover the qualities that constitute *supervisory style*, a term she had often heard in practice but whose meaning was nebulous. By analyzing interviews with 20 experienced supervisors about their "general approach to supervision," Dr. Friedlander and a colleague (Friedlander & Ward, 1984) constructed parallel versions of the Supervisory Styles Inventory, which revealed, in cross-validated factor analyses, the multidimensionality of *style*: Whereas the "attractive" style reflects the supervisor's friendliness, warmth, and supportiveness, the "interpersonally sensitive" style reflects the supervisor's perceptiveness, intuitiveness, and commitment, and the "task oriented" style reflects a style that is didactic, prescriptive, goal-driven, and evaluative.

Recognizing that all three supervisory styles reflect desirable approaches to the supervision process, Dr. Friedlander turned her attention to complications in the supervisory relationship, which led to several investigations of role conflict (Friedlander, Keller, Peca-Baker, & Olk, 1986; Ladany & Friedlander, 1995; Olk & Friedlander, 1992) and conflictual supervisory relationships (Nelson & Friedlander, 2001). All of this relationally focused research, which reflected her personal experience over the years of supervising beginning trainees in master's and doctoral practica, culminated in the critical events model, which she and colleagues developed to conceptualize and study the specific strategies, interventions, and behaviors that constitute an explicitly interpersonal style of supervision.

*Lee Nelson*: Dr. Nelson is and has always been a teacher. Across professional settings, from high school to community college to university environments, she has taken profound satisfaction from assisting with the intellectual and emotional development of her students. Her primary motivation for pursuing a PhD in psychology was the promise of training psychotherapists and counselors. Moreover, her research interests have always been directed toward understanding and improving training relationships and conditions. Thus, from the beginning of her doctoral level career, she pursued training in and research on the supervision process.

As a graduate student she involved herself primarily with Elizabeth Holloway's work on coding supervision process, understanding how factors such as supervisor theoretical orientation and sex of supervisor and supervisee influence the interplay of power and involvement in the supervision interaction. This work impressed upon her the importance of implicit messaging in supervision and psychotherapy. As a student of interpersonal/relational theory, she recognized that a supervisor's messages, both explicit and implicit, have the power to influence supervisee behaviors with clients and patients through the parallel process. She adopted the adage (which she regularly teaches): "Do unto others as you would have them do unto others." A highly evaluative, controlling supervisor will beget an evaluative, controlling therapist. Through advanced training in psychoanalytic psychotherapy, Dr. Nelson began to hone her skills as a therapist and supervisor, with a sharp focus on the process, as well as content, of her clinical interactions. She is also a scientist and can't help but interrogate most definitions that are placed before her. She has come to realize that the "magical" term *parallel process*, wherein experience is passed from therapy relationships to supervision relationships and vice versa, is nothing more than an example of the behavioral foundation of Bandura's social learning process. We "try on" what we see modeled.

In the 1990s Dr. Nelson was influenced greatly by the concept of reflectivity and involved herself with Susan Neufeldt's work on how it occurs in supervision. Dr. Nelson believes that assisting supervisees to reflect (i.e., spend time becoming aware of and learning about how they interact with clients and patients and how to use their interactions) is a key element of supervision. Thus, when she teaches supervision, she emphasizes the reflective process and how to facilitate it.

Because she became a supervisor at a time when the research literature on supervision was scant, Dr. Nelson's most profound early influence came from Mueller and Kell's (1972) classic text *Coping With Conflict*. They addressed the natural conflict inherent in supervision as a function of the therapeutic, yet evaluative, nature of the relationship, arguing that resolution of this natural conflict is a key challenge in the supervisory process. This notion has always influenced Dr. Nelson's work, as both a supervisor and a supervision researcher. Her later work has focused on how supervisors and supervisees experience conflict and how excellent supervisors go about preventing and mitigating negative outcomes of conflict with supervisees. Through observation of and reflection on the supervision process, excellent supervisors directly address interpersonal tensions, take ownership of their contribution to the tensions, and work to repair supervisory alliance ruptures. Dr. Nelson's interest in the approach to this text and in the companion DVD described earlier stems from her strong conviction that a key skill in quality supervision is the ability to identify and address explicit, as well as implicit, sources of conflict in the relationship.

# 1

# Overview of the Critical Events Model

**Supervisor:** ... Elise,[1] what other cases do you need to talk about today?

**Supervisee:** (*hesitantly*) Well, I did get a message from Frank—remember the new client I saw last week? (*pause*) He said in his message that he wouldn't be keeping any future appointments—that he's not ready for therapy yet.

For the supervisor, this is a choice point. Should he ask Elise more about this client and, if so, should they discuss whether a follow-up phone call is necessary *or* should they discuss what occurred—or failed to occur—in the intake session that led to the client's decision not to return for therapy? Alternately, should the supervisor focus on Elise, the supervisee, whose hesitancy in disclosing the client's decision suggests some

---

[1] With the exception of Tiffany (see Chapter 5), all case examples used throughout this book are composites and have been disguised to protect confidentiality.

http://dx.doi.org/10.1037/14916-002
*Supervision Essentials for the Critical Events in Psychotherapy Supervision Model,* by N. Ladany, M. L. Friedlander, and M. L. Nelson

discomfort? If so, is Elise simply uncomfortable with the client's decision to drop out or is she also uncomfortable revealing the client's decision to her supervisor? Ideally, all of these issues should be addressed. The dilemma is which path to take—where to start and toward what end.

Supervisors often face choice points like this one when working with novice supervisees, as well as with more advanced supervisees in practicum or internship, and even with experienced, postdegree psychotherapists. How a supervisor decides which path to follow is highly contextual. That is, the decision depends not only on the supervisee's training level but also on other characteristics of the supervisee (e.g., skill level, degree of self-awareness, openness), factors related to the clinical setting (e.g., institutional policies, length of the waiting list), factors related to the supervision itself (e.g., the duration and strength of the working relationship, the congruence of their theoretical approaches to clients) and, of course, factors related to the client and his personal circumstances.

Choice points like this one make psychotherapy supervision challenging. One option that many supervisors take, especially when they and their supervisees carry a large client caseload and time is limited, is simply to prescribe how to handle the case. Taking this approach, the supervisor in this situation might say something to Elise like, "That's too bad. We can certainly find you another new case for next week. Meanwhile, close out his chart and write him a letter, encouraging him to call for another appointment in the future if he changes his mind." This authoritarian, case management approach fulfills the oversight function of supervision but does little to further the supervisee's development of professional competence.

In contrast, the supervisor who takes an interpersonal, or process-oriented, approach to supervision is doing more than overseeing her supervisee's cases. Rather, in interpersonal supervision there is a dual focus—not only is the supervisor helping the supervisee to develop professional competencies by discussing his or her work with clients, but also he or she is modeling these competencies within the supervision relationship itself. Moreover, it is precisely this responsive attunement to both client and supervisee that makes supervision rewarding as well as challenging. The challenge is in managing the back-and-forth focus, for which at times the supervision relationship is in the foreground and the therapeutic work is in the background, and at other times the therapy takes center stage, with the supervision relationship in the background. Supervision is particularly rewarding when it all comes together: when a supervisee recognizes precisely how to use his or her positive experience with a supervisor to inform the kind of relational experience he or she is striving to develop with clients.

In this book, we take a close look at how the intertwined supervisory and therapeutic relationships can help supervisees become responsive counselors, social workers, and psychotherapists. We call our interpersonal approach to supervision a critical events model because our focus is on working through the kinds of issues that are commonly problematic for supervisees. In this contextual model, supervision—like psychotherapy—is seen as evolving through successive tasks whose cumulative impact, successful or not, determines the ultimate outcome. Some supervision tasks, such as initiating the relationship ("getting to know you") and defining the goals and parameters of supervision, tend not to be problematic. However, when a dilemma or an impasse arises—either within the supervision relationship itself or in the supervisee's work with one or more clients—the resolution of that dilemma or impasse takes center stage. The complexity arises when resolving the critical event necessitates a shift in focus from the therapeutic relationship to the supervision relationship or vice versa.

Our objective in developing the critical events model was to provide supervisors and supervisors in training with guidelines and illustrative examples for resolving commonly occurring critical events in psychotherapy supervision. The next sections of this chapter provide an overview of the model in general terms.

## THE EVENTS PARADIGM: A CONTEXTUAL APPROACH

Since the 1970s, theory and research on the supervisory process has burgeoned in all of the mental health disciplines. Unfortunately, the literature has not provided the kind of knowledge that supervisors need for their actual, day-to-day work with psychotherapy supervisees. It is generally understood that the overarching purpose of supervision is to develop professional competencies (Falender & Shafranske, 2004), including learning to be attuned and responsive to clients (Friedlander, 2012, 2015), accurately conceptualizing clients' problems (Blocher, 1983), applying a variety of empirically supported treatment approaches, and developing client-specific treatment plans (Bernard & Goodyear, 2014). Despite this common understanding of the goals of supervision, how and under what conditions these objectives can best be accomplished has not been established in the supervision literature.

Although little is known about how to get from point A to point B in a supervision session, we do have some general knowledge, broadly construed, about effective and ineffective supervision (Ellis et al., 2014). For example, research has shown that role conflict can be detrimental to the supervisory relationship (Ladany & Friedlander, 1995; Nelson & Friedlander, 2001) and that to avoid conflict, experienced supervisors work to be explicit about supervisees' role expectations throughout the supervision process (Nelson, Barnes, Evans, & Triggiano, 2008). We also know that supervisees especially value working with "interpersonally sensitive" supervisors (Friedlander & Ward, 1984, p. 541; Shaffer & Friedlander, 2015), and that strong supervisory alliances play a role in supervisees' satisfaction with supervision (e.g., Ladany, Ellis, & Friedlander, 1999). More pertinent process questions are still unanswered, for example: How do effective supervisors minimize role conflict, and how do they behave in session to address ruptures in the supervisory alliance? How and under what circumstances do interpersonally sensitive supervisors address their supervisees' personal difficulties?

We can begin to answer questions like these by considering the context of supervisory processes: that is, what it means—on a behavioral level—to be a responsive supervisor (Friedlander, 2012, 2015). Responsiveness requires a different approach when the supervisee is a novice and feels "over her head" versus when the supervisee is fairly advanced and has similar feelings. Responsiveness requires behaving differently with a supervisee who made an egregious ethical violation versus with one who is in the midst of a personal crisis. Responsiveness requires behaving differently depending on whether or not a supervisee has consciously been seductive in response to a client who is sexually provocative.

As humans, we are naturally contextual. That is, we make decisions and act based on our appraisals of each successive context that we encounter. As supervisors, to be maximally responsive to our supervisees, we need a wealth of contextual information—about the culture, the setting, the client, the supervisee, and more—to inform our actions. To decide how to handle challenging supervisory situations, such as how to address an ethical violation with a supervisee or how to work with a problematic supervisee, supervisors need a set of guidelines to recognize and then evaluate the dilemma to choose the most effective strategy in a particular context.

The events paradigm offers supervisors some guidelines to choose what needs to be discussed in supervision (the content) as well as the kinds of sequential, interpersonal behaviors that can bring about change (the process). By viewing the supervisory process as a series of meaningful events with specific, definable tasks and goals, supervisors can select the interpersonal strategies that have the greatest possibility of resolving challenging situations.

## VIEWING PSYCHOTHERAPY AND SUPERVISION AS A SERIES OF TASKS WITHIN EVENTS

In both supervision and psychotherapy, there are meaningful steps along the way to problem resolution: steps that can be anticipated, planned for, carried out, and then evaluated. It may require several (or many) sessions to achieve a single objective, such as working through a trauma (therapy) or learning a new clinical technique (supervision), and within a therapy or a supervision session more than one objective can be addressed.

Let's start by considering the process of psychotherapy. Over time and as a therapist gains clinical experience with diverse clients, she or he begins to think about the process of change in chunks—phases, if you will—rather than seeing it as a discontinuous blur of questions and answers, facts, and suppositions. The therapist comes to feel the rhythm of a session as well as the rhythm of change. The therapist can see herself or himself working on something specific within a session and coming back to it in a different way over the course of treatment. The therapist also learns that, occasionally, something occurs that is particularly powerful—the "aha" of the client's insight or a poignant moment of intimacy—an event that moves the therapy forward in new and potentially unexpected ways.

Perceiving the therapeutic process as a sequence of events occurs naturally with time and with clinical practice. As they gain experience, therapists begin to think about each session, or portion of a session, as an episode in a story. Each episode or event has a beginning, middle, and end, in which one or more specific "tasks" are worked on and, it is hoped, accomplished. In other words, therapists do not make moment-by-moment decisions about the ultimate path to follow to arrive at the ultimate therapeutic goal, such as to reduce the client's depression. Rather, these momentary decisions are informed by a sense of how to accomplish the task at hand, be it to assess the client's motivation for change, make it safe for the client to discuss troubling feelings, or review the client's gains to date. It is simply unrealistic to work any other way.

In other words, psychotherapy is made up of proximal (e.g., feel safe discussing troubling feelings), intermediate (e.g., make new social connections), and distal (e.g., reduce depression, enhance life satisfaction) goals. Similarly, supervision is made up of proximal (e.g., examine expectations for the practicum), intermediate (e.g., learn how to end therapy sessions on time), and distal (e.g., enhance professional competence) goals. And as in psychotherapy, obtaining these goals requires the accomplishment of a series of tasks that are worked on episodically.

To illustrate, consider the earlier example with Elise, the supervisee whose client, Frank, decided to drop out after the first session. The primary, distal goal of supervision with Elise, to learn to be a competent psychotherapist, is not addressed globally in any one supervision session. Rather, the supervisor has proximal and intermediate goals. In Elise's case, the intermediate goal may be to learn how to handle dropouts, and more generally to learn how to motivate clients to engage in psychotherapy or to learn how to address a client's resistance. To achieve each of these intermediate goals, the supervisor and supervisee work on specific "tasks" within and across supervision sessions by discussing one or more specific clients. Working on the goal of learning how to address resistance, the first supervisory task might be for Elise to understand Frank's decision to drop out. The task would be carried out by reviewing Frank's history and closely reviewing the intake session. Then, after coming to some understanding of Frank's decision, the next supervision task might be in service of an intermediate goal, to conceptualize client resistance—in general terms—from several theoretical perspectives. Finally, in yet another supervision episode, working on the intermediate goal of addressing client resistance, the task might involve role playing a session in which Elise addresses a client's ambivalent motivation for change.

In the events paradigm, the identification of, the working through, and the accomplishment of a specific task—in other words, the task analysis— are essentially what defines the event. Events in supervision are common and predictable, just as they are in psychotherapy. For example, when the supervisory relationship begins, the initial event typically is devoted to the goal of developing a supervisory alliance, with the associated tasks of getting to know one another, clarifying the roles and expectations for supervision, and reviewing agency policies. Generally when supervision ends, the final task involves evaluating the supervisee's professional competencies.

Some supervision textbooks discuss important common tasks, but in this book we focus specifically on critical events in supervision: events that tend to be particularly challenging for both supervisee and supervisor. Each chapter offers guidance in the form of a task analytic process model for resolving different dilemmas in supervision. However, before discussing this model of supervision in more detail, it is important to understand the origins of the task analytic model. The next section provides a more detailed description of task analyses in psychotherapy and supervision.

## THE TASK ANALYTIC MODEL

During the past 20 to 30 years, the events paradigm for researching interpersonal behavior in the psychotherapy context has taken hold in the literature. Although there are various approaches to studying meaningful therapy events, the most common is called *task analysis.* Applying the approach of industrial psychologists for defining, studying, and measuring the accomplishment of tasks in a work environment, psychotherapy researchers study tasks within critical events in individual as well as couple and family therapy. In short, task analysis is a rational–empirical method for using theory and clinical wisdom to develop and investigate a conceptual model of interaction with a specifiable, in-session outcome.

As explained earlier, the task analytic model assumes that therapy (and supervision) consists of tasks to be accomplished or dilemmas to be resolved, and the cumulative process of accomplishing these tasks within a supportive relationship results in good outcomes. To illustrate, a psychotherapy event might involve the task of understanding a client's "problematic reaction" (Rice & Saperia, 1984, p. 29) to something that occurred in her life. Another therapy event might involve resolving some kind of intrapsychic conflict (Greenberg, 1983) or unfinished business (Greenberg & Foerster, 1996) that a client identifies. All of these—exploring problematic reactions, intrapsychic conflicts, or unfinished business—are important tasks that often are addressed in therapy because they are what therapy is about.

Of course, the kinds of tasks to be worked on in therapy depend on the client's circumstances and the therapist's theoretical approach. However, some tasks are common for virtually all clients and therapists, regardless of the setting, theoretical approach, or problems being addressed. For example, different therapists and clients, in different settings and with different issues, might need to clear up a misunderstanding between them (Rhodes, Hill, Thompson, & Elliott, 1994) or repair a rupture in their relationship (Safran & Muran, 1996).

Despite commonalities across therapies, a particular task may be approached differently depending on the particular therapeutic system involved. For example, in individual therapy, a common task is exploring symptoms. Typically, a cognitive–behavioral therapist would explore a client's symptoms quite differently than would a psychodynamically oriented therapist, even though understanding a client's symptoms is a meaningful proximal goal for both therapists.

An important aspect of task analysis is that "successful" events—the point in the session or sessions during which the task at hand is resolved or accomplished—are assumed to proceed similarly, with the caveat that differences in the process can have important practical implications. Here is another point where individual differences and context come into play. Take, for example, the task analytic study of "sustaining engagement" events in conjoint family therapy (Friedlander, Heatherington, Johnson, & Skowron, 1994). In this study, task resolution was defined as a behavioral shift such that family members who initially were reluctant to engage with one another in solving a specific problem broke through their impasse and began actively discussing and working on the problem together. In this study, in all of the "unsuccessful" events but in none of the "successful" ones, the families were headed by single parents. This observation suggests that the task analytic model that the researchers discovered might be valid only for two-parent families; different processes may be involved when therapists try to encourage "sustained engagement" in single-parent families (Friedlander et al., 1994).

A final consideration is that successfully resolved tasks require a strong interpersonal relationship. How a therapist or supervisor addresses a given task may vary depending on the stage of the working relationship and the degree to which the alliance is solid. Because the processes of change in therapy and supervision tasks often involve challenge, clients and supervisees alike need to see the social context as safe, a place to take risks and grow.

Typically, a task analysis begins with identifying an event, such as the portion of a session when a misunderstanding arises between supervisor and supervisee, and its related task (in this case, resolving the misunderstanding). The event and associated task should be ones that are common occurrences and ones that can bring about change in the client or supervisee. A common example in psychotherapy is a rupture in the therapeutic alliance (Safran & Muran, 1996) and its corollary in the supervisory alliance (Friedlander, 2015). In both contexts, the task of "repairing" a ruptured alliance is essential to providing the client/supervisee with an important, new relational experience that allows the therapy/supervision to progress more smoothly.

Whether the context in which critical events occur is psychotherapy or supervision, the task analytic model has three basic components: marker, task environment, and resolution (Greenberg, 1986). First, in the context of supervision, the marker is a statement or behavior on the part of the supervisee that signals a need for work on a specific task. The marker often is a single statement, such as Elise's response to her supervisor's question about what client they should talk about next: "Well, I did get a message from Frank. . . . He said in his message that he wouldn't be keeping any future appointments—that he's not ready for therapy yet." The marker might also be a segment of dialogue that lasts several minutes or a behavior that the supervisor notices and considers important to address, such as when a supervisee is chronically late to her supervision sessions. In the first instance, Elise's comment "marks" the need to discuss her client's decision to drop out after the first session. In the second instance, the supervisee's chronic lateness "marks" the need to discuss expectations or ground rules for supervision.

Second, the task environment includes the "performances" on the part of the client/supervisee and the "operations" (Greenberg, 1986) on the part of the therapist/supervisor. Performances and operations refer to the steps along the way to accomplishing the task at hand: for example, understanding a client's decision to drop out or eliciting and then negotiating expectations for supervision. These steps along the way are the various interactional sequences that promote the successful accomplishment of the task. In the case of the chronically late supervisee, the interactional sequences within the task environment might involve exploring the supervisee's feelings about being supervised, focusing on the supervisory alliance (goals, tasks, bond), attending to parallel processes (perhaps the supervisee's client is always late to the therapy sessions), and/or evaluating the supervisee's professional attitudes.

Finally, the resolution, which occurs at the end of the event, refers to the outcome or accomplishment of the task at hand. A successful resolution reflects a new understanding, an integration of conflict, a plan for action, and so forth. By definition, the lack of a resolution means that the task has not been accomplished. In unsuccessful events, the task environment lasts until either the focus of conversation changes or the session itself ends. In the case of Elise, a successful event might involve a better understanding of Frank's decision to drop out and a new understanding of how to assess a client's motivation for change in an intake session. In the case of the chronically late supervisee, a successfully resolved event might involve a new understanding of the need for supervision and the supervisor's expectations.

## IDENTIFYING CRITICAL EVENTS AND TASKS IN SUPERVISION

Although supervision has many commonalities with therapy, it can be distinguished in three major ways: It is evaluative, it is not voluntary, and it is explicitly educational (Ladany, 2013). Because supervision has a unique set of interpersonal dynamics, specific elements in the supervision process are necessarily different from those that characterize the psychotherapy process. For this reason, the identification and research of task analytic models of supervision should be qualitatively different from task analytic models of psychotherapy.

In developing the task analytic model of critical events in supervision, we integrated our clinical experience as supervisors with extant theory and research on supervision. Our intent was to develop an approach that would be heuristically appealing and practically meaningful for supervisors and supervisors in training, and we anticipated that researchers could use the model to study significant mechanisms of change in the supervision process. Essentially, the model is like a template for identifying and researching critical supervision events. We chose the various events discussed in this book (e.g., role conflict, skill deficits) because they tend to occur frequently and are particularly challenging. However, there are many other supervision events that could be identified and researched using our task analytic template (Ladany et al., 2005).

Before illustrating the model more fully, we would like to lay out our assumptions. First, our process model is pantheoretical. Consequently, a supervisor working with a supervisee who wants to develop her mindfulness skills for conducting acceptance and commitment therapy can use our model as readily as a supervisor working with a supervisee whose interest lies more within the psychodynamic tradition. Similarly, the task analytic model applies to supervision of counseling and psychotherapy within any professional discipline—psychology, psychiatry, marital and family therapy, social work, mental health counseling, school guidance, or nursing. Our second assumption is that the model is explicitly interpersonal. As mentioned, we view interactions and relationship as central to working through critical events in supervision. A third assumption is our belief that an emphasis on supervisees' learning, growth, and development requires more than case management. We do not see case management as the sole, or even primary, purpose for supervision, and we do not consider the supervisor to be a "trainer" in the sense of directing or evaluating a therapist's adherence to a manualized treatment. The fourth assumption, as explained earlier, has to do with our view of the supervision process as a sequence of meaningful events or episodes, each of which has an identifiable beginning, middle, and end. Although many events begin and are completed within one session, some events necessitate two or more supervision sessions, and some are interrupted and returned to later. Finally, we assume that the events we selected to highlight in this book are critical ones: that is, they are challenging and have implications for achieving important supervision goals.

In brief, a task analysis refers to the process of addressing specific critical events that tend to occur in supervision and are important for supervision outcomes, and the term task refers to what the supervisor is attempting to accomplish in a specific critical event. For instance, one critical event is the portion of a supervision session devoted to discussing a supervisee's countertransference; the task within the event is to better understand the countertransference and how to use it to clinical advantage with the client. As we discuss in more depth in the following section, the marker, task environment, and resolution, the three phases in the task analytic process model, are embedded within the supervisory working alliance. In Figure 1.1, the task analytic process model of supervision is illustrated.

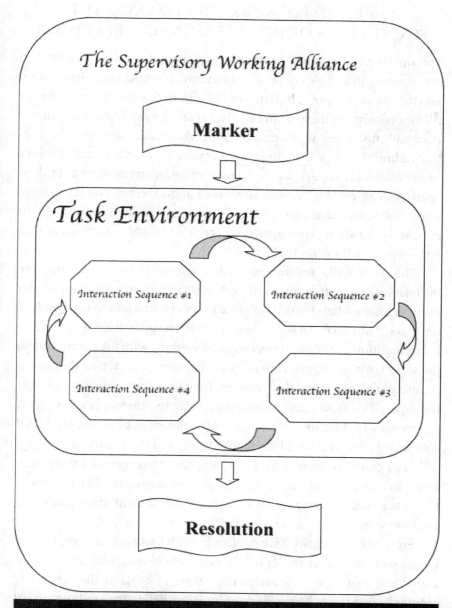

## The Supervisory Working Alliance

**Marker**

## Task Environment

Interaction Sequence #1

Interaction Sequence #2

Interaction Sequence #4

Interaction Sequence #3

**Resolution**

### Figure 1.1

Prototypical critical event in supervision. Adapted from *Critical Events in Psychotherapy Supervision: An Interpersonal Approach* (p. 12), by N. Ladany, M. L. Friedlander, and M. L. Nelson, 2005, Washington, DC: American Psychological Association. Copyright 2005 by the American Psychological Association.

## SUPERVISORY WORKING ALLIANCE: THE FOUNDATION OF INTERPERSONAL SUPERVISION

The working alliance, one of the most frequently studied constructs in the supervision and psychotherapy literature, is arguably the foundation for effective supervision. In terms of definition, the supervisory working alliance consists of three components: (a) an agreement between supervisor and supervisee on the goals of supervision, such as improving specific technical skills, enhancing the supervisee's conceptualization ability, or increasing the supervisee's awareness of countertransference in therapy; (b) an agreement between supervisor and supervisee on the tasks of supervision, such as focusing on the supervisee's feelings toward her clients; and (c) a strong emotional connection or bond between supervisor and supervisee (Bordin, 1983).

The alliance, like any interpersonal relationship, grows over time. For the relationship to strengthen rather than falter, supervisor and supervisee must negotiate what should take place in supervision and to what end. To illustrate, if one goal of a supervisee's practicum supervision is to enhance his recognition of countertransference in working with his clients, he and the supervisor must agree, either implicitly or explicitly, that this goal is meaningful. They must also agree on how to accomplish the goal (i.e., the supervision tasks), such as reviewing tapes together and exploring the supervisee's feelings toward every client with whom he or she works. Of course, various tasks could be chosen to expand the supervisee's recognition of countertransference, but unless the supervisee and supervisor agree, to a meaningful extent, on how this awareness should come about (i.e., what should occur and when), the accomplishment of the goal could be compromised.

From the perspective of the alliance, it can be assumed that impasses of one sort or another reflect implicit or explicit disagreements between supervisor and supervisee about the nature of goals or the process of accomplishing them. These kinds of impasses define the kinds of critical events we describe in subsequent chapters of this book.

The importance of the supervisory alliance is well documented. Studies have shown that a favorable supervisory alliance is predictive of supervisees' competency with multicultural issues (Ladany, Brittan-Powell, & Pannu, 1997); effective evaluation (Lehrman-Waterman & Ladany, 2001); flexibility in terms of collegial, interpersonally sensitive, and task-oriented supervisory styles (Ladany, Walker, & Melincoff, 2001); facilitating supervisees' self-disclosure (Ladany, O'Brien, et al., 1997); supportive gender-related events (Walker, Ladany, & Pate-Carolan, 2007); liking for the supervisor (Melincoff, 2001; Melincoff, Walker, Tyson, Muse-Burke, & Ladany, 2001); supervisee self-efficacy (Efstation, Patton, & Kardash, 1990); and satisfaction with supervision (Ladany, Ellis, & Friedlander, 1999; Shaffer & Friedlander, 2015). On the other hand, an unfavorable supervisory alliance is related to supervisees' experiences of role ambiguity and role conflict (Ladany & Friedlander, 1995); nondisclosure of relevant material (Ladany, Hill, Corbett, & Nutt, 1996); insecure attachment (Riggs & Bretz, 2006); negative supervisory experiences (Ramos-Sánchez et al., 2002); anxiety (Mehr, Ladany, & Caskie, 2015); and vicarious traumatization (Fama, 2003). Moreover, supervisees tend to view the supervisory alliance as unfavorable when they see their supervisors behaving unethically (Ladany, Lehrman-Waterman, Molinaro, & Wolgast, 1999; Nelson & Friedlander, 2001).

Highlighting the importance of the alliance in working through critical events, some research indicates that supervisees tend to rate the alliance unfavorably when they have experienced gender discrimination (Bertsch et al., 2014; Walker et al., 2007) or other counterproductive incidents in supervision (Gray, Ladany, Walker, & Ancis, 2001). At times, impasses in supervision originate not in disagreements about the goals and tasks but in the quality of the emotional bond. Like the working alliance in psychotherapy, the bond is crucial to the supervisory alliance and reflects the extent to which the supervisor is responsive to the supervisee's evolving needs (Friedlander, 2012, 2015). A strong bond is characterized by mutual liking, warmth, trust, and respect. Arguably, the quality of the emotional bond is a limiting factor in the extent to which a supervisor can suggest or impose challenging supervision goals and tasks.

Because the bond is strengthened when the supervisor is responsively understanding and empathic (Friedlander, 2015), the importance of empathy in supervision cannot be overstated. Unfortunately, many supervisors may be highly empathic psychotherapists but lack the same level of caring concern for their supervisees, especially when an impasse occurs between them. The bond can be compromised when a supervisor's zeal leads her or him to overlook or misjudge a supervisee's vulnerability in the face of a poor evaluation or a disagreement between them. Like clients, supervisees need supportive reassurance to accept and eventually to assimilate critical feedback. It is daunting for supervisees to feel disdain from their supervisors when those very supervisors speak about their own clients with compassionate concern.

In our interpersonal model of supervision, the supervisory alliance is the foundation for working through critical events, just as the therapeutic alliance is the foundation for challenging clients to change. As mentioned, we construe the supervisory and the therapeutic alliances as reflective of one another in a figure/ground configuration, where at times the supervisory alliance is the focus of the session (the figure) and the supervisee's alliance with her or his client(s) is not under discussion (i.e., the ground). At other moments, the supervisory alliance is not under discussion (the ground); rather, the focus (or figure) is the supervisee's relationship with her or his client(s).

Typically, the supervisory alliance is the figure early on in supervision. The alliance also becomes the figure when conflicts—impasses or ruptures—surface in the relationship. At other moments in supervision, the strength of the alliance fluctuates depending on the event at hand. In the context of a strong supervisory alliance, a supervisor is likely to be effective in challenging his or her supervisee, but when the alliance is weak, challenges may be seen as harsh or even insulting. When a supervisee seems overwhelmed or distressed by what is taking place in a supervision session, moving the supervisory alliance from the ground to the figure is essential. Depending on the supervisee's level of confidence or self-efficacy as a therapist, it may be helpful for the supervisor to "check in" with the supervisee about their relationship before proceeding to discuss the supervisee's work with specific clients. Repeatedly failing to "check in" with a vulnerable supervisee could well damage the supervisory work and, ultimately, the professional development of the supervisee.

## Identifying the Marker

In the task analytic model, the marker initiates the event at hand. Simply put, the marker refers to a statement, a series of statements, or a behavior that "marks" the supervisee's need for a specific kind of response on the part of the supervisor. Just as the marker in a therapy event signals to the therapist that a particular issue (i.e., task) needs to be addressed, such as the client's resistance to completing homework assignments, the marker in a supervision session signals to the supervisor that a particular action or focus is needed at that moment.

Sometimes the marker is readily apparent, such as when a supervisee directly asks the supervisor for help with a particular client or the supervisee brings up a professional concern or a desire to practice a specific technical skill. At other times, the marker is more subtle and thus easily overlooked. In other words, the marker may not be what the supervisee says or even what she or he does, as much as what she or he does not say or does not do. Some examples include arriving late to supervision, coming unprepared to discuss any clients, or repeatedly failing to record therapy sessions. In group supervision, the marker might be a consistent lack of participation in the group or a sarcastic response to feedback from a peer. The marker might also involve an interaction with a client that the supervisor observes in a recording of the supervisee's session. The marker might also be a defensive posture when certain topics are on the table in supervision, such as when the supervisor inquires about the supervisee's case notes. In these situations, it is crucial for the supervisor to tread lightly to avoid a rupture in the supervisory alliance, which will only complicate the successful resolution of the critical event.

Although different markers may indicate similar problems, different problems can manifest themselves with similar markers. As an example, role conflict (Chapter 2) could be "marked" by the supervisee's passive withdrawal in the supervision session, coming late to supervision appointments, or continually failing to record her therapy sessions. Yet these same markers might not be indicative of role conflict with the supervisor but rather the supervisee's need to recognize and understand a parallel process (Chapter 4). In some situations, the marker phase of the critical event can be prolonged. This phase does not end until the supervisor is clear about precisely what needs to be addressed at that point in the session.

## THE TASK ENVIRONMENT: WORKING THROUGH THE EVENT

After the marker is understood by the supervisor, the task environment takes center stage. Essentially, when broken down into its three parts, the task environment (see Figure 1.1) is a series of interactional sequences that are both the supervisor's operations (interventions or strategies) and the supervisee's performances or reactions (cf. Greenberg, 1986). Although the sequences that make up a task environment differ for different critical events and depend on the supervisee's readiness for change and developmental level as a professional, there are some common interactional sequences that characterize a distinctly relational approach to supervision (Shaffer & Friedlander, 2015), including sequences that reflect the processes of exploration, clarification, and working through. For example, in a countertransference event, the interactional sequences in the task environment most likely involve exploration (of the therapy relationship and the supervisee's feelings), a direct focus on the countertransference (clarification), followed by an interpretation and working through of the parallel process (Ladany et al., 2005).

Table 1.1 defines 11 interactional sequences that can characterize the operations and performances within the task environment of a critical supervision event. Naturally, these sequences are not mutually exclusive (a focus on countertransference usually involves exploration of feelings), and the list is not exhaustive of all possible sequences that characterize critical supervision events.

A recent program of research with these interactional sequences (Shaffer & Friedlander, 2015) showed that five of the 11 sequences constitute a single, relational factor. In other words, five key sequences were identified empirically as being most purely relational: focus on countertransference, exploration of feelings, focus on the therapeutic alliance, attend to parallel process, and focus on the supervisory alliance. In two studies, these five sequences (based on a sample of supervisees' frequency ratings on a new

## Table 1.1

## Common Interaction Sequences in the
## Task Environments of Critical Events

| Sequence | Definition |
|---|---|
| Focus on the supervisory alliance* | Discussion of aspects of the relationship related to agreement on the tasks and goals of supervision (including evaluation), as well as to the emotional bond between supervisor and supervisee. May either be a "checking in" about the alliance or an explicit discussion about what is taking place or should take place in supervision, including a focus on the supervisee's or the supervisor's feelings about their relationship. |
| Focus on the therapeutic process* | A discussion about what is taking place between the supervisee and client (i.e., the kinds of interactions that occur, the strength of the therapeutic alliance, and how the client sees the supervisee's behavior in relation to self and *vice versa*). |
| Exploration of feelings* | Typically, but not exclusively, a here-and-now focus. Feelings can be expressed about the client, the therapeutic relationship or process, about the supervisee's progress in training, or about personal issues. |
| Focus on counter-transference* | Discussion of how and why the supervisee's feelings and/or personal issues are "triggered" by a client's behavior or attitude. |
| Attend to parallel processes* | A discussion that draws attention to similarities between a specific therapeutic interaction and the supervisory interaction. Parallel processes may originate in either interaction and be mirrored in the other. |
| Focus on self-efficacy | A discussion of the supervisee's sense of confidence in his or her therapeutic skills (either specifically or globally), sense of self as a professional, or ability to function in various roles (e.g., as therapist, student, supervisee, colleague). |
| Normalizing experience | A discussion of how the supervisee's experience (either as a therapist, colleague, or supervisee) is typical and developmentally expected or appropriate. |
| Focus on skill | Discussion of the how, when, where, and why of conceptual, technical, and interpersonal skills. May include role playing or a discussion of how to apply theory to specific therapy interventions. |
| Assessing knowledge | Evaluating the degree to which the supervisee is knowledgeable in areas relevant to the cases(s) under discussion. Knowledge bases include ethics, research, and theory as applied to practice. |
| Focus on multicultural awareness | Discussion of the supervisee's self-awareness in relation to individuals who are similar and different in terms of gender, race, ethnicity, age, sexual orientation, religion, disability, family structure, or socioeconomic status. |
| Focus on evaluation | Discussion of the supervisee's performance in therapy, in supervision, and as a professional. May involve a discussion of feedback, critical and positive, either summative or formative. |

*Note.* *Interactional sequences in the Relational Behavior Scale (Shaffer & Friedlander, 2015). Reprinted from *Critical Events in Psychotherapy Supervision: An Interpersonal Approach* (pp. 15–16), by N. Ladany, M. L. Friedlander, and M. L. Nelson, 2005, Washington, DC: American Psychological Association. Copyright 2005 by the American Psychological Association.

measure, the Relational Behavior Scale [RBS]), were uniquely predicted by supervisors' "interpersonally sensitive" style of working with supervisees. Moreover, RBS scores were significantly associated with (a) a strong supervisory alliance and (b) supervisees' positive experience of the supervisor in the session in which relatively more RBS behaviors occurred. Taken together, these results strongly support the theoretical underpinning of the critical events model.

In the chapters that follow, we turn our attention to the interactional sequences that we believe are most likely to result in a successful resolution of the critical events under discussion. The 11 interaction sequences may be carried out in various ways depending on a variety of contextual factors, including gender, culture, personality/style, the supervisee's developmental level, the clinical context, state of the supervision relationship, and so forth. For this reason, the sequences for each event described in the following chapters are suggested but not prescribed ways for resolving critical events. Moreover, the kinds of sequences or interventions that a supervisor chooses to use within each interaction sequence of the task environment may differ from the interventions of another supervisor. For example, when using the sequence exploration of feelings, one supervisor might ask the supervisee how he or she felt when the client was silent for an extended period of time, or the supervisor might ask the supervisee to describe his or her experience of the client as they watch a portion of the recorded session together. Alternately, a supervisor might use different interventions with different supervisees. With a focus on countertransference, the supervisor might ask one supervisee if he or she ever felt similarly with people in his or her personal life, and in working with a different supervisee, the supervisor might inquire directly about other clients or what his or her emotional reactions bring to mind. In a gender misunderstanding event, when the supervisor is using the assessing knowledge sequence, she or he might ask the supervisee to take a feminist perspective on the client's life story. In a skill deficit event, the supervisor's focus on skills might involve role playing or asking the supervisee to explain why she or he used a particular intervention at a particular time.

We also want to point out that the various sequences in a task environment are not altogether discrete and at times the process is a recursive one (note the arrows between the various interactional sequences in Figure 1.1). What is consistent, however, is the continuous forward movement through the task environment toward some kind of "working through," which optimally leads to a successful resolution of the task at hand.

To illustrate, in Figure 1.2 the marker for a managing sexual attraction event is the supervisee's comment that she feels attracted to her client. Once the supervisor recognizes this marker as signaling a sexual attraction event, the task environment proceeds through the four interactional sequences of exploration of feelings, focus on the supervisory alliance, normalizing experience, and focus on countertransference, with their recursive nature indicated in Figure 1.2 by arrows. To illustrate the process model, Figure 1.2 depicts a linear progression of stages, but in actuality the order of these stages—and even their nature—is likely to differ based on a complex interaction of supervisee, supervisor, client, clinical setting, and strength of the supervisory alliance.

## THE RESOLUTION: THE END OF A CRITICAL EVENT

When all elements of the task environment come together successfully, the event ends with a resolution, the proximal outcome of the specific supervisory task at hand. Successful resolutions reflect an enhancement in (a) self-awareness, (b) knowledge, (c) skills, or (d) the supervisory alliance. By *self-awareness*, we mean the supervisee's recognition of precisely how her or his own prior life experiences, expectations or biases, feelings, behaviors, and/or beliefs influence her or his work with clients. *Knowledge* has to do with the theoretical, empirical, and practical understanding that a supervisee gains through graduate training and clinical experience. *Skills* refers to interpersonal, technical, or conceptual capabilities related to psychotherapy; they range from micro skills (interventions such as reassurance, asking open questions, making summations, and reflecting feelings) to complex therapeutic skills (e.g., conducting an empty-chair dialogue). The *supervisory alliance* refers to enhancing the emotional connection between supervisor and supervisee, coming to an agreement on supervisory goals and tasks, and/or addressing a rupture in the supervisory working relationship.

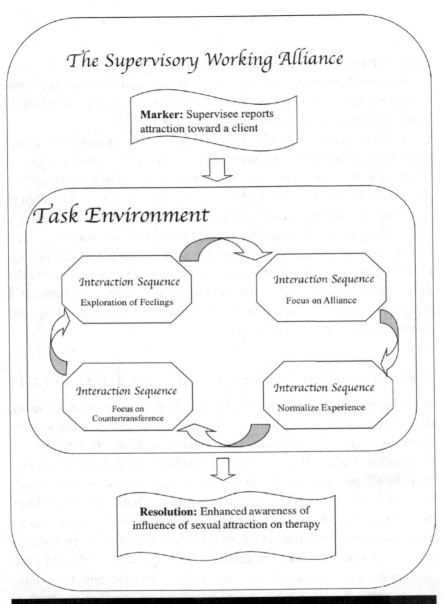

The Supervisory Working Alliance

**Marker:** Supervisee reports attraction toward a client

Task Environment

*Interaction Sequence*
Exploration of Feelings

*Interaction Sequence*
Focus on Alliance

*Interaction Sequence*
Focus on Countertransference

*Interaction Sequence*
Normalize Experience

**Resolution:** Enhanced awareness of influence of sexual attraction on therapy

## Figure 1.2

Example of a sexual attraction event. Adapted from *Critical Events in Psychotherapy Supervision: An Interpersonal Approach* (p. 17), by N. Ladany, M. L. Friedlander, and M. L. Nelson, 2005, Washington, DC: American Psychological Association. Copyright 2005 by the American Psychological Association.

The exact nature of any resolution is closely linked with the task at hand in a given supervision event. Thus, a resolution might involve greater self-awareness (in a countertransference event, for example) or planning for action (e.g., in a multicultural awareness event). Essentially, the resolution involves coming back to the original concern or point of entry into the event, signaled by the marker. In short, events with successful resolutions are those in which the task at hand is accomplished. For example, in a successfully resolved countertransference event, the supervisee has a new appreciation for his or her emotional reactions to the client in light of his or her own personal background or experience and explains to the supervisor a new strategy for working with the client in light of this new self-awareness.

Of course, not all tasks are successfully resolved. Those that are partially resolved or that are unsuccessful tend to lack closure. Clearly unresolved tasks are those in which the supervisory session ends with tension, anger, or withdrawal. In other situations, the event's conclusion may be less clear, such as when the supervisee agrees to follow the supervisor's suggestions but does so without a clear commitment or when the supervisor addresses the supervisee's feelings but, sensing resistance, shifts the conversation to another topic altogether. A poor conclusion to a critical event can be just as unsettling for a supervisee as it is for a psychotherapy client and arguably for the supervisor as well.

## Identifying Critical Events

Although the literature on critical events in supervision is limited, authors have written about some important recurring themes in psychotherapy supervision, many of which are universal. From this literature and our own experience as supervisors, we previously identified 10 critical events, with the following tasks: remediating skill difficulties and deficits, heightening multicultural awareness, negotiating role conflicts, working through countertransference, managing sexual attraction, repairing gender-related misunderstandings, addressing problematic attitudes and behavior (Ladany et al., 2005), facilitating supervisee insight, enhancing career counseling skills, and facilitating a corrective relational experience

(Ladany, 2006; Ladany et al., 2012; Ladany & O'Shaughnessy, 2015). In this book, we add working through parallel processes as an additional critical event. Although this list is by no means exhaustive, these kinds of tasks tend to be the most common and challenging ones that take place in psychotherapy supervision.

What can be particularly challenging is when one event leads to another event, which needs to be resolved before returning to working through the original one. For example, a session that begins with a countertransference event ("marked," for example, by a supervisee's comment that she or he feels "angrier than [she or he] should" toward a new client) could well turn into a role conflict event after the supervisor asks the supervisee to consider the personal basis for the strong reactions. If the supervisee feels that the supervisor's inquiry is personally intrusive, this rupture in the supervisory alliance needs to be repaired before there can be a successful resolution to the original countertransference difficulty with the client.

Alternatively, what begins as a critical event in supervision, say the supervisee's "problematic attitude" after receiving directive feedback from the supervisor, might well turn into a critical event related to the supervisee's therapeutic work with clients. This switch might occur, for example, if in discussing her or his general lack of confidence as a therapist, the supervisee discloses that her or his client has made sexual overtures to the supervisee. In a more critical situation like this one, it would be important to focus on the sexual attraction event within the therapy before returning to a discussion of the supervisee's problematic attitude in supervision (i.e., one trumps the other).

In this book, we focus on one-on-one, face-to-face supervision, although critical events clearly also take place in group supervision. Each chapter begins with research and theory relevant to the critical event under discussion. Next, we suggest a conceptual model for addressing each kind of event, in which the supervisory task at hand is marked by various possible behaviors or comments on the part of the supervisee. As described earlier and illustrated in the foregoing figures, each process model contains a marker, task environment (with suggested interactional sequences), and resolution. Following the description of each model are abbreviated transcripts that illustrate successful or unsuccessful task resolutions. Alongside the dialogue are the participants' perceptions, intentions, and reactions as the event is ongoing. At the conclusion of each chapter, we discuss some special considerations, which are noteworthy issues that may arise in working through each kind of critical event.

## FINAL THOUGHTS BEFORE VENTURING FORWARD

As we explained earlier and continue to emphasize: Context is key. That is, critical supervisory events do not occur in a vacuum. Like clients and therapists, supervisors and supervisees bring to the table a variety of backgrounds, personal experiences, and salient concerns that result in an exciting, yet sometimes bumpy, process of supervision. To capture the complexity of these contextual dynamics, our illustrative cases have varying characteristics of supervisors and supervisees, settings, and formats of therapy and supervision. In this way, we have strived to demonstrate the wide application of our model in hopes of encouraging readers to consider the diversity of supervision practice across fields of specialization.

One important point needs to be stressed at the outset. Supervisees are expected to come to supervision with an openness to the supervisory process and with at least rudimentary skills, knowledge of psychotherapy processes, and some degree of self-awareness. When a supervisee lacks these essential characteristics, it behooves the supervisor to recognize the supervisee's shortcomings as soon as possible in their work together so as to address them responsively and responsibly. Sometimes this can be done as a critical event but other times, such as when a supervisee lacks even rudimentary skills, could involve remediation before clinical interactions occur.

We realize that the personal/emotional aspect of supervision tends to be poorly understood by beginning supervisees, and the process of self-discovery can be threatening even for experienced supervisees. For this reason, a crucial aspect of supervision is clarification of role expectations at the outset. Indeed, informed consent for supervision that includes clear role expectations is required (see *Guidelines for Clinical Supervision in Health Service Psychology*, American Psychological Association, 2014) to circumvent role conflict or ruptures in the supervisory alliance. Clarification of expectations is essential so that from the outset, the supervisee understands and agrees that his or her personal concern or background may become a focus of the supervision conversation, but the goal of such a conversation is not to change the supervisee's personality structure or to work through his or her personal problems. Rather, the goal of this kind of supervision conversation is to address specific personal barriers that may be impeding the supervisee's work with clients or hindering his or her productive participation in supervision.

Any discussion of professional behavior should be conducted with a clear delineation of professionalism. Although this book is not an ethics casebook, our case descriptions and discussions may well raise pertinent ethical issues. For this reason, we encourage supervisors to consider their respective professional ethical codes and guidelines.

We believe that good supervision of good therapeutic work is good supervision of good therapeutic work, regardless of whether it is called *counseling* or *psychotherapy*. For this reason, we use the term *supervisee* rather than *trainee* to include postdegreed practitioners who are receiving supervision. For ease of reading, we vary the gender of supervisor and supervisee, but in all cases the choice of gender is arbitrary. Further, because we believe that the field's differentiation of "counseling" from "psychotherapy" is neither precise nor meaningful, we use the term *psychotherapy* for purposes of consistency. Ultimately, we acknowledge the richness of the many professional disciplines in which the supervision of psychotherapy is provided and researched.

## 2

# Ambiguity and Conflict in the Supervision Relationship: It's All About the Roles!

Arguably, nowhere is there a greater need for supervisor responsiveness than when there occurs a break, or rupture, in the supervisory working alliance (Friedlander, 2015). In contrast to the critical events we have discussed thus far—skill deficits and problematic attitudes and behavior—critical events involving the supervisor's and supervisee's respective roles in their relationship can take center stage even when there is no ongoing discussion of clients. To complicate matters further, role conflicts can overtake a conversation about the supervisee's clinical work in the blink of an eye. Ignoring the conflict will likely make the supervision process quite tense and uncomfortable for both parties. At its worst, failure to resolve a role conflict can irretrievably damage the supervisory alliance and negatively affect the welfare of the supervisee's clients (cf. Nelson & Friedlander, 2001; Ellis et al., 2014).

http://dx.doi.org/10.1037/14916-003
*Supervision Essentials for the Critical Events in Psychotherapy Supervision Model*, by N. Ladany, M. L. Friedlander, and M. L. Nelson

What do we mean by *role conflict*? This term and a similar construct, *role ambiguity*, were adapted from industrial/organizational psychology to the context of psychotherapy supervision by authors who pointed out that, like workers in any job environment, supervisor and supervisee need clear and unambiguous guidelines for their respective roles, both in relating to one another and in carrying out their job tasks (Friedlander, Keller, Peca-Baker, & Olk, 1986). Role ambiguity occurs when a worker is unclear, unsure, or confused about what her or his supervisor expects. Role conflict, on the other hand, occurs when the supervisee has specific expectations for herself or himself and/or the supervisor, but these expectations contradict those of the supervisor. The Role Conflict and Role Ambiguity Inventory (Olk & Friedlander, 1992) offers specific examples of role conflict (e.g., "My supervisor told me to do something I perceived to be illegal or unethical and I was expected to comply") and role ambiguity (e.g., "I was not certain about what material to present to my supervisor") in supervision.

It is easy to see that role ambiguity is most likely to occur with novice supervisees, who come to supervision for the first time or who are being supervised in a clinical setting (such as an inpatient psychiatry unit) that is new for them. Indeed, research with the Role Conflict and Role Ambiguity Inventory supports this supposition (Olk & Friedlander, 1992). In contrast, because by definition role conflict occurs when supervisee and supervisor have opposing expectations for what is to take place between them, critical events related to role conflict are most likely to surface with relatively more advanced supervisees.

Consider, for example, a supervisee whose previous supervisors focused only on case management or how to follow an evidence-based treatment manual. When the supervisee's new supervisor asks about the supervisee's personal experiences with racial discrimination, the supervisee is distressed because he has no idea how such a highly personal discussion could possibly advance his clinical skills. As another example, a supervisee, new to conducting conjoint family therapy, is hesitant to disclose her outrage with the parents in one of her cases because she is worried that the supervisor would see her as incompetent and thus unsuited to work with the family.

The resolution of ambiguity is a fairly straightforward process of clarifying expectations, but the resolution of conflict is more complex and arguably more challenging. At the very least, resolution of a role conflict involves direct communication about the opposing expectations and it often involves backtracking, clarifying intentions, disclosing personal material, compromising, and apologizing. All of these processes are difficult enough for people to engage in when they share social power, but in the supervision relationship there is an unambiguous hierarchy, and the evaluative, gate-keeping function of supervision is ever present, particularly in the minds of supervisees. For this reason, role conflict in supervision can be pernicious.

In the following sections, we illustrate and discuss critical events related to role ambiguity and role conflict. The markers for each kind of event can show up in the context of a discussion about what should take place in supervision or in the midst of a conversation about the supervisee's work with one or more clients. When conflict or ambiguity events begin in the absence of a specific clinical discussion, they tend to be marked by behavior on the supervisee's part that reflects his or her expectations (or lack thereof) for the supervision process, such as being chronically late or coming to supervision unprepared, when his or her paperwork (clinical reports, process notes) is incomplete, or when he or she requests something specific of the supervisor (e.g., "Do you want to review my tapes before we meet each week?"). More often, however, these kinds of events are initiated within the context of a clinical discussion.

In the three examples that follow, we pick up on the supervision of Elise (from Chapter 1), whose client dropped out after their first session. Using the same supervisee in all three examples, we begin with an illustration of a successfully resolved role ambiguity event, followed next by two role conflict events, one that is unsuccessful and one that has a successful resolution (see Figure 2.1).

## EXAMPLE OF A SUCCESSFULLY RESOLVED ROLE AMBIGUITY EVENT

### Marker

**Supervisor:** So what other cases do you need to talk about today?

**Supervisee:** [*hesitantly*] Well, I did get a message from Frank—remember the new client I saw last week? [*pause*] . . . He said in his message that he

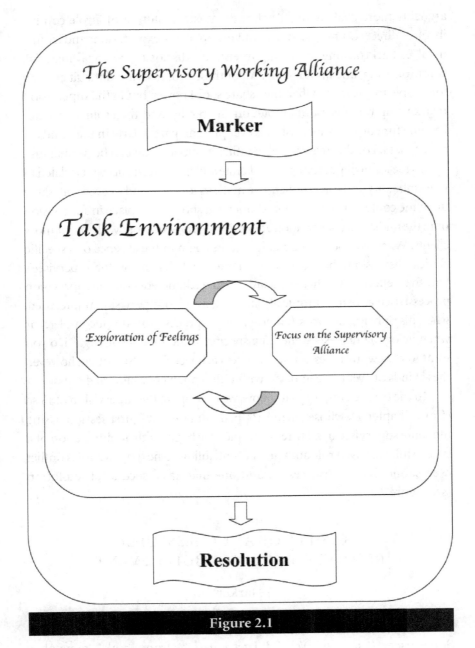

*The Supervisory Working Alliance*

**Marker**

*Task Environment*

*Exploration of Feelings*

*Focus on the Supervisory Alliance*

**Resolution**

**Figure 2.1**

Process model of a role conflict event.

wouldn't be keeping any future appointments—that he's not ready for therapy yet. [*realizes she needs to discuss this client but unsure what to focus on; worried about being seen as lacking for having lost the client*]

**Supervisor:** Any ideas on why he dropped out? [*unsure whether to focus on Elise's feelings or on her intake skills*]

**Supervisee:** I'm not sure. . . . Should I go get the tape of my session with him for us to look at together? [*wants to please the supervisor*]

**Supervisor:** We could do that. Would that be most useful for you at this point? [*still searching for a focus*]

**Supervisee:** I don't know. [*pause*] It *might* be, but I don't know. . . . Is it okay that I don't have a good reaction to it all? [*realizes she should bring up some negative feelings she's having about the case*]

At this point, the marker is evident. Elise is stymied by what she should talk about in supervision related to a client whom she will no longer be seeing. She is unclear whether expressing her feelings about the client is appropriate or even if doing so would be helpful, and because she is frustrated (perhaps even angry) at the client, she is unsure whether her reaction is justified and, even if it is, whether the supervisor wants to—or should—hear about it.

## Task Environment

The supervisor has now recognized that Elise's hesitance has to do with not knowing what he expects of her in supervision. He judges that the issue is Elise's lack of understanding of the supervision process and her role as a supervisee in deciding which of several paths to follow to be of most benefit to her learning. Responsive to what he views as Elise's ambiguity about how they should work together most productively, the supervisor sees this moment as an opportunity to consider her expectations and subsequently to clarify his own expectation that Elise take more initiative in supervision.

### Exploration of Feelings

**Supervisor:** Elise, are you saying you're wondering whether we can talk about your feelings toward Frank? And maybe your feelings about *any* client? [*focusing on the supervisory alliance by clarifying Elise's expectations*]

**Supervisee:** Yes, I guess I am. I know I need to think about just why he dropped out *and* what I did wrong in the intake. I don't know what's most important. [*still trying to please as well as to communicate her lack of understanding of what's expected of her by the supervisor*]

**Supervisor:** All of these are, potentially! I want to let you know, though, that I very much welcome a discussion about your feelings toward your clients, even if they *have* dropped out unexpectedly, like Frank did. After all, as therapists, *we* can't be helpful if we're not aware of our strong reactions, don't you think? [*chooses to ignore Elise's self-blame in favor of clarifying his view of the supervisory process and also putting himself in her shoes (i.e., modeling and normalizing her experience)*]

**Supervisee:** Yes! I agree. I just didn't know where you wanted me to start. [*explains her need for more direction*]

### Focus on the Supervisory Alliance

**Supervisor:** Actually, let's put feelings about Frank aside for a moment and talk about how supervision should go from each of our perspectives. It's understandable that you're concerned about this. [*focuses on the supervisory process, normalizing Elise's experience of supervision*]

**Supervisee:** Right. The only other supervisor I had just wanted to review all my cases. I guess I got the impression from her that I should keep my feelings out of it. I wasn't sure what you thought about that. [*still fearful of asking directly for what she wants, not knowing if her need to examine her feelings is an appropriate topic for supervision*]

**Supervisor:** Well, I'm glad you mentioned it, then. A therapist's feelings toward a client are critically important in my view, regardless of whether you're doing experiential therapy or CBT. So that's where I'm different from your previous supervisor, I suppose. [*reinforces Elise's disclosure of the source of her anxiety*]

**Supervisee:** Great. [*feeling somewhat reassured*]

**Supervisor:** But there's a larger issue here, not just whether or not to focus on your feeling reactions to your clients. I'd like *you* to be the one to decide where we should start as we talk about any one of your cases. With Frank, for example, I could see it being just as helpful to discuss your feelings as to review what went on in the intake. Or, actually, we could get to your feelings by doing that. [*clarifies his expectation that Elise take more charge of their discussion*]

**Supervisee:** Yes, I can see that! Of course. But [*pause*] . . . what if we just focus on my feelings and then I might not know what I did wrong with him? [*tentative, worrying that she might make the wrong choice*]

**Supervisor:** You can leave that worry to me. I'm not suggesting that you do *all* the deciding about what we focus on, and rest assured that if I think you've missed something important, I won't be shy about bringing it up! (*smiling*) [*reassures her that the supervision process is a shared responsibility*]

## Resolution

**Supervisee:** Yeah, I'm glad of that. [*feels somewhat relieved of the pressure to figure out what needs to be discussed*]

**Supervisor:** For example, I'm not even so sure that you did anything "wrong" with Frank. Didn't his voice message say that he wasn't ready for therapy "yet"? [*responsive to Elise's potential for self-blame*]

**Supervisee:** Right, it did.

**Supervisor:** So maybe part of my job will be to point out to you what you might be mistakenly blaming yourself for? [*further clarifying his role*]

**Supervisee:** (*laughs*) Well, that's a relief!

**Supervisor:** (*laughs*)

**Supervisee:** So, what I think I'd like to do now is tell you how upset I am about Frank dropping out. [*feeling empowered to direct their discussion*]

**Supervisor:** (*smiles*) Let's go for it! [*reinforces Elise's initiative*]

In this successfully resolved event, the supervisor recognized that role ambiguity, rather than passivity, was behind Elise's reluctance to decide how to discuss her case in supervision. In recognizing the marker for role ambiguity, the supervisor was well aware that Elise was a beginning supervisee and that she had had little prior experience either as a therapist or as a supervisee.

Yet the dialogue could well have led to an alliance rupture caused by role conflict if the supervisor had seen Elise's hesitance as a characterological problem rather than simply as uncertainly about what was expected of her in supervision. In the next example, we illustrate how differently the discussion may have played out if Elise's role ambiguity were misunderstood by the supervisor as passivity.

## EXAMPLE OF AN UNRESOLVED
## ROLE CONFLICT EVENT

### Marker

**Supervisor:** Any ideas on why he dropped out?

**Supervisee:** I'm not sure. . . . Should I go get the tape of my session with him for us to look at together?

**Supervisor:** We could do that. Would that be most useful for you at this point?

**Supervisee:** I don't know. [*pause*] It *might* be, but I don't know. . . . Is it okay that I don't have a good reaction to it all?

**Supervisor:** Your reaction to Frank is one thing, but I'm stymied by your lack of preparation for our discussion. I can't help but wonder if Frank's dropping out might have something to do with your not being fully prepared for *him* either. [*frustrated at what he sees as Elise's passivity and wants her to see the potential parallel in her clinical work*]

**Supervisee:** (*silent*) [*feels criticized, silenced*]

**Supervisor:** Okay, let's review your intake with Frank. [*decides to take charge, thinking he can show Elise how passive she was with her client*]

**Supervisee:** Okay. [*upset, yet willing to go along with the supervisor's direction*]

While at this point Elise is feeling personally attacked, the supervisor is unaware of her feelings toward him, instead viewing her as becoming increasingly passive in their interaction. What started out as role ambiguity for the supervisee has now become role conflict. That is, Elise expected the supervisor to decide where to focus their discussion, but he has now challenged her competence by indicating that she was not prepared for the intake with her client. The interaction between them has become fairly tense.

**Supervisor:** So, can you recap what happened in the intake with Frank? [*feeling increasingly frustrated, believing that a focus on the therapeutic process will be more productive*]

**Supervisee:** He began, right from the beginning of the session, giving me his entire life history, which is full of trauma. His brother shot both his parents when he was a teenager, and then Frank was sent to live with some relatives he didn't know very well. [*unsure what to discuss, decides to present the client's issues*]

**Supervisor:** Wow, what a story! Has he ever had treatment before? How did you end the session? [*quite disturbed to hear this history, thinking that the client might be ambivalent about entering therapy; decides to assess how well Elise handled the client's ambivalence and whether she discussed the potential value of therapy given all the trauma the client revealed*]

**Supervisee:** I don't know what you mean. We *did* make an appointment for this week. [*trying to avoid being criticized again yet not understanding what he means about how she "ended the session"*]

**Supervisor:** I mean, did you talk with him at all about what it might mean to open up all these old wounds of his in therapy? [*even more frustrated with Elise at this point, thinking that he will give her a hint about what she should have done in the intake*]

**Supervisee:** I guess I didn't. [*feels chastised*]

**Supervisor:** So it's not surprising that he decided not to commit to treatment. [*wanting to make a point*]

**Supervisee:** I guess so. [*aware of the supervisor's frustration and believes that he expects her to own her error*]

**Supervisor:** What have you learned from this? [*trying to assess Elise's ability to reflect on her experience*]

**Supervisee:** I guess I should have talked with him about how hard therapy might be and see if he really wanted to start, if he really wanted to relive what happened to him as a child. [*decides that she needs to agree with him to avoid being criticized further*]

**Supervisor:** Exactly. [*satisfied, believing that she has now seen her error*]

Here the rupture to the alliance is quite evident, with the supervision session becoming increasingly tense. However, the supervisor does not recognize the marker of a role conflict event. The supervisor is frustrated with Elise, and she is feeling judged harshly, perhaps unfairly, by the supervisor. When the supervision session began, she needed support and encouragement to air her frustration about losing the client, as well as some space to begin to understand what may have gone wrong or what she might have done differently in the intake with this client to assure his commitment to treatment. At this point, realizing that the supervisor is quite concerned about the client's welfare, Elise decides to redirect their interaction to be more in line with what she perceives the supervisor expects from her.

**Supervisee:** Do you think I should call him back? I could bring up some of these issues or at least let him know that he can come back if he wants to. [*trying to figure out what he wants her to do*]

**Supervisor:** What do *you* think would be best? [*wanting to empower Elise, beginning to realize that he has been somewhat critical*]

**Elise:** I'm afraid that if I do that, he won't say anything. I really don't think he is ready to talk about all that happened to him. [*taking a risk by offering her perspective on the client's resistance*]

**Supervisor:** So why don't you write him a letter, letting him know that you got his message and that he's welcome to come back to the clinic in the future. [*decides to take charge, thinking that continuing the discussion of this client is not likely to be productive, that he should just tell Elise what is needed in line with clinic policy*]

**Elise:** I can do that. I *will* do that. [*wanting to be compliant, then realizing that to please him, she needs to sound more self-assured*]

The supervisee is highly aware of being judged and found lacking. She is confused about how or if she can turn the situation around with her supervisor, and right now she is only interested in doing what she thinks he expects her to do. This role conflict event is thus unresolved. Because the supervisor did not recognize the marker, the event never proceeded to a task environment. Although he did focus on the supervisory alliance, there was no successful resolution. Rather, the supervisor simply moved on.

**Supervisor:** Why don't we talk about another case, one that is ongoing? [*deciding that it will be more productive to switch gears and discuss a case that Elise feels better about*]

**Supervisee:** Sure. Which one of my clients do you want to hear about? [*relieved that she no longer needs to discuss the client who dropped out*]

Elise continues to try to please her supervisor, having decided that he has an agenda that she needs to figure out to please him. While relieved that they have moved off the previous topic, she is feeling frustrated and hurt by what has taken place so far between them. Her intention at this point is simply to get through the rest of the hour without letting the supervisor see her distress. And she has no idea what to do with her client.

In this vignette, the role conflict event was unresolved. Supervisor and supervisee went on to discuss another client, with their unease with one another continuing to shadow the remainder of the supervision session and, perhaps, subsequent supervision sessions.

What makes this event a role conflict rather than simply a conflict? In an event that involves resolving an overt conflict, there is a clear disagreement ("I think . . ." versus "I disagree. I think it's . . ."), whereas in a role conflict event there is tension, generally covert, because each person expects something different to occur in the relationship with the other person. In the current example, Elise expected support from the supervisor and to receive guidance to understand why her client may have dropped out and what she could learn from this unfortunate experience. The supervisor, on the other hand, expected Elise to take ownership of the supervision process by initiating a clinically rich discussion of her clients and clearly asking for what she needed from supervision.

Because of the contradictory expectations, the supervisor became quite frustrated with the supervisee, and as his frustration grew, he became more convinced that the problem was Elise—namely, her passivity and lack of clinical skill. Not only did he not recognize the marker for role conflict, but also he was unaware of how his own behavior and attitude were contributing to the growing rupture in their alliance. Although well aware of his own discomfort and somewhat aware of Elise's discomfort, he had no idea that he contributed to the rupture in his approach to the supervisee by blaming her for being unprepared for supervision and equally unprepared for her session with the client. Unfortunately, as Elise became more submissive, the supervisor became more direct and dominant, which only served to increase her submissiveness. Unfortunately, the gender dynamics in this event played a significant role, as the combination of male supervisor/female supervisee along with the power dynamics of supervision often result in a supervisee being silenced and feeling unable to please the supervisor or "get it right" (Friedlander, Blanco, Bernardi, & Shaffer, in press).

Later, when the supervisee related the client's extreme trauma history, the supervisor judged her even more harshly. Understandably, his focus shifted to worrying about the client's welfare in the wake of what he now concluded to have been a poorly conducted intake. However, note that he learned little about what had taken place in the therapy session. When we look closely at the dialogue, we see that Elise, criticized by the supervisor for being unprepared and feeling upset that she had apparently mishandled the intake, actually provided minimal information about the case.

All told, the supervisee learned little from this supervisory session other than she had made a grievous error with her client and that her supervisor was demanding and hard to please. It is highly unlikely that Elise, feeling judged, would address the rupture in the supervisory alliance, regardless of how uncomfortable she felt. What is likely is that without a repair, the course of supervision from this point onward will be unpleasant for both parties. Indeed, a rupture in a supervisee's working alliance with a client is all too easily replicated in the supervisory alliance, particularly when the supervisor becomes so concerned about the client that he fails to be responsive to the supervisee (Friedlander, 2015). This is precisely what happened in this case.

## EXAMPLE OF A SUCCESSFULLY RESOLVED ROLE CONFLICT EVENT

As depicted in the following illustration of this same case, the five most "purely" relational sequences in our model are an obvious choice in a role conflict event. Moreover, no critical event other than role conflict—and perhaps countertransference—is more likely to necessitate use of the most clearly relational of our 11 sequences. Indeed, any of the other events we have identified in this book can "turn into" a role conflict event if supervisor and supervisee have contradictory expectations for their roles in the supervisory process.

Now, let's reconsider Elise's supervision. This time, rather than see Elise's increasingly submissive responses as being attributable to her passive character or poor clinical skills, the supervisor recognizes her hesitant and submissive responses as a marker of role conflict.

### Marker

**Supervisee:** Do you think I should call him back? I could bring up some of these issues or at least let him know that he can come back if he wants to.

**Supervisor:** What do *you* think would be best?

**Supervisee:** I'm afraid that if I do that, he won't say anything. I really don't think he is ready to talk about all that happened to him.

**Supervisor:** So why don't you write him a letter, letting him know that you got his message and that he's welcome to come back to the clinic in the future.

**Supervisee:** I can do that. I *will* do that.

At this point, with discussion of the client seemingly concluded, the supervisor recognizes the marker of a role conflict event. Deciding to work toward a resolution of this rupture to their alliance, the supervisor shifts focus, and the task environment now begins.

## TASK ENVIRONMENT

### Focus on the Supervisory Alliance

**Supervisor:** [*pause*] Leaving Frank's case aside for the time being, I'm thinking that we should perhaps talk about what's going on now, between us two? [*tentatively suggests a focus on the supervisory alliance*]

**Supervisee:** Okay . . . ? [*somewhat wary*]

**Supervisor:** I'm feeling uncomfortable about how our discussion has been so far today. Do you feel it too? [*modeling immediacy, realizing that Elise is unlikely to bring up her feelings without his "permission" to do so*]

**Supervisee:** I guess. . . . Yes, I *do* feel uncomfortable. I'm not sure why, though . . . ? [*feeling bold enough to agree that she's uncomfortable as well*]

**Supervisor:** Well, I'm thinking that you've gotten quieter and I've gotten more directive. It's not the way I'd like it to go between us, ideally. I'd much rather you take the lead in orienting our discussion. [*states his own expectation in hopes that Elise will do the same, carefully labeling behavior "quieter" so as to avoid making her more uncomfortable*]

**Supervisee:** Yes, you said that earlier. [*feeling the need to say something but unsure how to respond*]

## Exploration of Feelings

**Supervisor:** Could you let me know your reaction to that? [*realizing that she's well aware of his behavior, exploring her feelings*]

**Supervisee:** Umm . . . [*pause*] Well, to be honest, I didn't feel so good about it. I mean, I did bring up this client at the beginning of supervision. I "took the lead" when I did that.

**Supervisor:** Yes, you did. [*responds minimally, hoping Elise will say more about what's bothering her*]

**Supervisee:** You said I was unprepared for supervision, just like I was unprepared for the client. But I *wasn't* unprepared for him. [*feeling defensive, reluctant to state her anger and hurt*]

## Focus on the Supervisory Alliance

**Supervisor:** So, that comment of mine is what started us off on the wrong foot today? [*seeks clarification of Elise's perceptions of the rupture; realizing she is not willing to label her feelings, describes the rupture in mild terms*]

**Supervisee:** Yes, I guess so. [*the words "started us off on the wrong foot" seem acceptable enough to admit to*]

**Supervisor:** I appreciate your frankness, Elise. Not easy to do! Before I put my foot in my mouth again (*both laugh nervously*), what were you hoping we'd talk about today? I'm not sure I communicated to you clearly enough my expectation that you come to supervision with what is most important to you each week. [*indirectly apologizes for his part in the alliance rupture and seeks to clarify their mutual expectations*]

**Supervisee:** Maybe not . . . but I did want to talk about my reaction to Frank and also to try to figure out why he decided not to come back. I think I expected something different. [*beginning to assert her disappointment in how the supervision session is going*]

**Supervisor:** From me? [*clarifies, realizing how hard it is for Elise to express her negative reaction to him*]

**Supervisee:** Well, yeah. [*hesitantly agrees but not secure enough to comment further*]

**Supervisor:** So you were expecting more support, not criticism from me. [*labels their discrepant expectations, using the word "criticism" to give her permission to indicate that she perceived his comment as critical*]

**Elise:** Yeah, exactly. [*beginning to relax a bit*]

### Attend to the Parallel Process

**Supervisor:** Hmm. . . . Well, I missed that; I certainly did. I'm having a strange thought right now though. . . . I'm wondering if you and Frank got off on the wrong foot, too, like you and I did today? [*draws attention to the ruptures in both alliances*]

**Supervisee:** (*pause*) That's interesting! What do you mean? [*quite curious now but also wary that she might be blamed*]

**Supervisor:** I jumped to some conclusions about you without checking them out. I assumed you wanted something specific from me but I didn't give you room to let me know, and you . . . [*owning his part in the rupture*]

**Supervisee:** (*interrupting*) . . . did the same thing with Frank! Wow! [*excited to see the parallel process*]

**Supervisor:** What are you thinking now? [*giving her space to express her understanding of the parallel process*]

**Supervisee:** Now that I think about it, I was so sure, from his history, that he'd want and *need* therapy, that I didn't give him the space to really consider what that meant, I mean to consider if he's ready to bring up all that past trauma from his childhood. [*expanding her ideas freely now, feeling bolder*]

**Supervisor:** And *I* was so sure about you! But I thought only about what *I* wanted and expected from you, not what *you* wanted and expected from me! [*continuing to own his part in their rupture*]

**Supervisee:** This is amazing! (*laughs*) [*genuinely relieved and hopeful that their relationship is now on better footing*]

**Supervisor:** Isn't it? (*smiles*) Why do you suppose we re-created it here? [*realizing from her laughter that Elise is now more comfortable, exploring her deeper understanding of the parallel process*]

**Supervisee:** I saw you as the "Supervisor," capital "S," and easily got intimidated because underneath I was worried that I'd really messed up with Frank. [*comfortable enough now to express her genuine worry about her competence*]

**Supervisor:** Yes, that fits! And Frank saw you as . . . ? [*continuing to explore Elise's understanding of the parallel process*]

**Elise:** He saw *me* as "Therapist," capital "T"! [*begins to enjoy the discussion*]

**Supervisor:** . . . and was intimidated? [*tentatively probing Elise's understanding of the client's experience of her*]

**Supervisee:** I guess so! [*no longer feeling defensive about her work with the client*]

**Supervisor:** And supervision, like therapy, *is* intimidating. Sometimes I forget that, since it's been so long since I was a grad student myself! [*owns his part in the rupture; by indicating that supervision is "intimidating," he takes the sting out of Elise feeling "intimidated" as a person*]

## Resolution

**Supervisee:** It's amazing how much better I feel now!

**Supervisor:** Me too! I'll try to give you more space in the future and not just assume you want something you may not want from me. [*modeling rupture repair*]

**Supervisee:** And I'll try not to get so easily intimidated by your questions! [*fully engaged at this point*]

**Supervisor:** Great—you'll use your voice, like you just did, I hope?

**Supervisee:** Absolutely!

In contrast to the previous, unsuccessful handling of the same event, the supervisor has acknowledged his role in the alliance rupture and that Elise's feelings of intimidation tend to be part and parcel of the supervision experience. Next, the supervisor calls Elise's attention to the parallel process (i.e., her "jumping to conclusions" about her client, Frank), which may have intimidated him, and the supervisor's "jumping to conclusions" about Elise's lack of preparation for supervision, a comment that clearly intimidated her. Both supervisor and supervisee were amused by this covert parallel process, and the ensuing lighthearted interaction suggests that their alliance has been restored. With a successful resolution to the event, they can now turn their attention back to discussions of Elise's clinical work.

As illustrated in both the role ambiguity and the role conflict events, problems in the supervisory relationship arise because of unclear or contradictory expectations for supervision on the part of the supervisee and supervisor. In the role ambiguity event, the supervisor recognized that Elise's submissive behavior toward him was contextual; that is, it was caused by a need for clarity about her expected role as a supervisee. By contrast, in the role conflict event the supervisor failed to consider the contextual influence of Elise's submissive behavior, considering it to be highly problematic not only in supervision but also in her clinical work. In the unresolved illustration, the supervisor raised Elise's defenses by implying that she was deficient, whereas in the resolved illustration, the supervisor attended directly to the supervisory alliance and demonstrated a willingness to reduce his social power by admitting his part in the rupture and acknowledging Elise's feelings of intimidation as part and parcel of being a supervisee.

## SPECIAL CONSIDERATIONS: ROLE AMBIGUITY AND CONFLICT IN GROUP SUPERVISION

Thus far in this chapter, we have considered only individual supervision. However, it is easy to see that in the context of group supervision, the potential for role conflict is heightened because of the multiple relationships that supervisees have with their peers. The flow of supervision can be easily disrupted when supervisees in a group have interpersonal difficulties with one another or different statuses, such as gender and race (cf. Friedlander et al., in press). In any group, clinical skills are likely to be unevenly distributed, and supervisees are likely to be highly aware of one another's strengths and weaknesses. For this reason, offering and receiving feedback to one another about clinical work can cause tension within the group, particularly when there are covert external forces (e.g., competition for assistantships) that are affecting their relationships or when they expect only to hear praise and confirmation from their peers.

Ruptures to the group alliance can also occur when the supervisor points out a supervisee's personal issues in a round-robin, "hot seat" kind of group process. For this reason, we suggest that in the absence of a strong sense of safety and clear norms for risk taking and confidentiality, supervisors should function primarily in their educative and collegial roles in the group, saving the therapeutic and evaluative functions of supervision for their individual relationships with supervisees.

Indeed, it is often the case that a supervisor works with supervisees individually as well as within a group. Role conflict can be particularly troublesome in this situation or in any situation in which there are dual relationships between supervisor and supervisee. It is common for supervisors in an academic program to have multiple relationships with their supervisees, whom they may teach in seminars, work with on research projects, or advise in an administrative capacity. It is particularly challenging (yet necessary) to separate these various roles.

We believe that it is essential for supervisors, more so than supervisees, to be highly mindful of the potential for role conflict so that they can explain the differing role expectations to their supervisees. Supervisees need to know that to keep the multiple roles distinct, it is advisable not to discuss course work or a research project during the supervision hour and not to refer to personal issues discussed during supervision (e.g., countertransference or vicarious traumatization) in other academic contexts.

## CONCLUSION

In other professions, the goals and processes of supervision tend to be straightforward and administrative, and the managerial and evaluative aspects of supervision tend to be clear to all parties. In the mental health field, however, a supervisor needs to strike a balance between ensuring client welfare and promoting the supervisee's professional growth. Unfortunately, at times these dual responsibilities are at odds.

Moreover, by its nature, clinical work places extraordinarily complex demands on supervisees and their supervisors. Supervisees tend to be highly sensitive to the intimate clinical material they hear in their daily work with clients, and their degree of openness and willingness to explore their reactions to this material has a strong influence on the ease and depth of the supervisory relationship. With support from supervisors and a nuanced and contextual understanding of the various role demands of supervision, supervisees can reap great benefit from fluid shifts in focus from their clients to themselves and back again.

# 3

# Addressing Skill Difficulties, Deficits, and Competency Concerns

One of the primary goals of supervision is to foster skill and competency development. Although acquiring basic therapeutic skills such as active listening and advanced empathy is challenging enough, competency is a vast umbrella encompassing areas of personal and professional growth, diagnostic and conceptualization ability, personal awareness, reflective practice, and professional demeanor (Fouad, 2014). Supervisors are responsible for monitoring all aspects of skill development and competency. Moreover, they are gatekeepers for the profession and charged with the challenging task of advising a supervisee to leave the profession if he or she is unable to demonstrate adequate levels of skill and competency. In this chapter, we address skill and competency development and the thorny issue of inadequate supervisee performance.

http://dx.doi.org/10.1037/14916-004
*Supervision Essentials for the Critical Events in Psychotherapy Supervision Model,* by N. Ladany, M. L. Friedlander, and M. L. Nelson

## "SKILLS" DEFINED

We conceptualize skill development within three primary domains: technical skill, interpersonal skill, and conceptual skill. Technical skills, including using appropriate body language and vocal tone, paraphrasing, labeling feelings, summarizing, and identifying meaning, are all taught to beginning therapists before they advance to meeting with clients. However, when beginners progress from role playing to seeing actual clients, the real test of their skill development begins. Thus, supervisors working with novice therapists must attend to their supervisees' ability to use the specific skills regularly and appropriately. Early practicum courses are where much supervision related to skill development takes place. Supervisors at this level are often in the instructor role, helping supervisees remember and practice the basic skills intentionally. Should a supervisee be unable to demonstrate the use of basic skills, even with the help of the supervisor's instruction and coaching, a skill deficiency may be present.

Although interpersonal skill certainly involves aspects of technical ability, the interpersonal domain incorporates aspects of the whole person of the therapist. Supervisees must recognize early on that they are expected to be interpersonally responsive. Their role is not simply to diagnose and treat a disorder; rather, it is to be psychologically and emotionally present in the room with a vulnerable human being. One might say that the ability to provide Rogers' (1951) facilitative conditions (unconditional positive regard, respect, and empathy) is the core of interpersonal skill.

Problems with skill acquisition may reflect skill difficulties *or* skill deficits. We view a skill *difficulty* as present when a supervisee is undergoing a developmentally appropriate challenge in learning a skill, whereas a skill *deficit* is present when a supervisee seems particularly immobilized in learning a skill. Supervisees at the advanced practicum level who fail to demonstrate skills they should have demonstrated earlier in training (such as rapport building) are of particular concern. Supervision focused on skill acquisition and demonstration of facilitative conditions involves support for the supervisee, modeling for the supervisee the conditions the supervisee must offer the client, and helping the supervisee embrace mistakes and ambiguity. All these strategies are aimed at addressing a supervisee's skill difficulty in the interpersonal realm. Should the supervisee seem unable to overcome initial performance anxiety or set aside her or his discomfort with ambiguity long enough to name emotions and stay present with the client's experience, the supervisor may be facing a skill deficit that requires more intense intervention and/or remediation.

# PROCESS MODEL:
# SKILL DIFFICULTIES AND DEFICITS

## Marker

Markers of skill difficulty include behaviors such as asking too many closed questions rather than open-ended ones; failure to reflect feeling, content, and meaning; providing premature reassurance; and failure to address cultural differences early in the counseling relationship. Other examples include persistently responding to clients in a friendly or chat-like manner, providing reassurance rather than empathy, and barraging clients with closed questions. Effective skills can be practiced and improved over time, provided a supervisee is open to learning and emotionally flexible.

The supervisor should suspect a skill deficit, however, when a supervisee seems unable or unwilling to practice the required behaviors. A marker of skill deficiency might show up later in a practicum or training sequence as evidence that the supervisee is unwilling or not ready to appropriate the necessary skills. A common marker of supervisee skill deficiency is the reply "That isn't me" in response to a supervisor's concern that after weeks or months of work, a skill is still not being demonstrated. A supervisee who claims that he plans to provide only one particular type of structured therapy, such as cognitive–behavioral (CBT) or reality therapy, may be attempting to hide his interpersonal deficits behind a mask of feigned professionalism that is intended to belie skill deficits. Such skill deficiency is a sign of the supervisee's cognitive and/or emotional rigidity, and that rigidity needs to be addressed.

## Task Environment and Resolution

As with many challenges in supervisee development, the interactional sequence focus on evaluation is necessary but not sufficient. The supervisee must understand precisely what type of skill is not present in her or his clinical work and that an inability to demonstrate the skill will result is unfavorable evaluation. For this reason many training programs require students to videotape their work with clients so that the skills supervisees are and are not demonstrating can be evaluated.

When a simple skill difficulty has been ruled out and it becomes clear that a skill deficit is present, it is critical to begin by identifying the source of the deficit. The task is to name the identified skill deficit and inquire about what underlies the deficit. It could be that the supervisee has simply not been able to operationally define the skill and translate it into observable behaviors. What does it mean to label feelings? Does the supervisee have an adequate feeling vocabulary? Is the supervisee confused about when to offer a reflection of feeling? Does she or he feel that it is inappropriate to "invade" the client's space by naming the client's feelings? Does the supervisee fear working with feelings based on a concern about becoming overwhelmed by them? Or is it that the supervisee defends against discussing feelings because it has historically been unsafe for him or her to do so?

Only when the root cause of the deficit has been uncovered can an appropriate supervision intervention be selected and implemented. In many cases, exploration of feelings may be necessary to understand what underlies a supervisee's difficulty using a particular skill. Moreover, a focus on the supervisory alliance may be called for if the supervisee becomes defensive in the process of receiving evaluative feedback from the supervisor.

Resolutions related to skill difficulties occur when the supervisee's behavior reflects learning and willingness to work with new skills. If a supervisee continues to resist the supervisor's attempt to help her develop particular skills, the skill difficulty event is considered unresolved (see Figure 3.1).

## EXAMPLE OF A SUCCESSFULLY RESOLVED SKILLS DEFICIT EVENT

Using the task analysis model described in the first chapter, we now describe an example of a technical skill deficit, rooted in the supervisee's lack of interpersonal skill, and the supervisor's approach to addressing the deficit. The following interaction takes place during a formative evaluation session wherein the supervisor gives direct feedback to a supervisee on her use of a specific skill: reflecting feelings. The supervisor is a White woman in her mid-50s with 25 years of therapy and supervision experience; the supervisee is an African American woman in her early 30s who is in her first practicum in a university setting. The supervision relationship is cordial and generally positive. Supervisor and supervisee already addressed their racial differences and agreed to discuss any issues that might arise in relation to those differences.

### Marker

The supervisor has repeatedly been having difficulty coaching her supervisee to use feeling statements. In this case, one marker is clear—a lack of feeling statements in the supervisee's responses to the client, as indicated on multiple behavioral tracking forms of therapy sessions. That the supervisee has been unresponsive to the supervisor's coaching is a second marker that signifies a skill deficit.

### Task Environment

#### Focus on Evaluation

**Supervisor:** So, as we have discussed over the past several weeks, I am still not seeing a lot of feeling reflections in your work. It may be time for us to have a discussion about this and what is making it hard for you to do that.

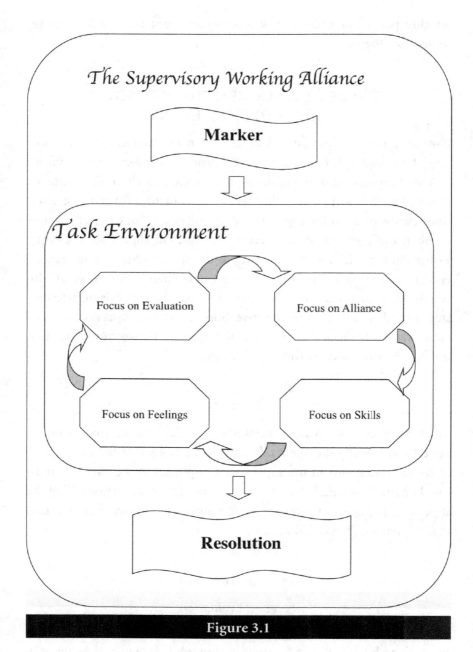

**Figure 3.1**

Process model for addressing a skill difficulty event.

I sense that you are really struggling to label your clients' feelings and am wondering what that is like for you. [*tries to deliver feedback while honoring the supervisee's experience*]

**Supervisee:** (*defensively*) I'm just not sure that feelings are important in therapy.

**Supervisor:** Can you tell me more about what you mean? [*elicits meaning*]

**Supervisee:** I think therapy should be about identifying goals and strategies to reach those goals. I am not sure about the value of feelings in therapy. I think we are there to help clients solve their problems, not to get involved in crying sessions. [*responds defensively*]

**Supervisor:** Okay. So you believe that identifying your clients' feelings and responding to them empathically may not be necessary for good therapy to take place. In fact you see getting into feelings as a waste of time. [*models reflection of content and meaning*]

**Supervisee:** Yes I do. I just can't understand why that is important.

Here the supervisor faces a choice point. She can delve into a conversation about why feelings are important in counseling, thus remaining on a cognitive level with the supervisee. Alternately, she can take a bolder step, moving toward addressing feelings within the supervisory relationship.

### Focus on Supervisory Alliance

**Supervisor:** It seems like it must be uncomfortable for you to talk about this with me. [*invites supervisee to focus on their relationship*]

**Supervisee:** Yes, because I don't dwell on feelings much. Life is like a series of puzzles to be solved, so I'd rather look at it that way. [*backing away from the invitation*]

**Supervisor:** So to be sitting here with me, a White supervisor who is bringing up feelings, really takes you out of your comfort zone in more ways than one. I mean, maybe it seems to you that I am trying to impose my White values on you . . . ? [*operating on a hunch, the supervisor speculates* *about racial difference as a source of tension related to working with feelings in supervision*]

**Supervisee:** That may be part of it. I mean, I had to grow up Black in a very White neighborhood and city. I never had the luxury of being able to have feelings in social settings because I had to appear competent and in control. I've never allowed myself to cry in front of White people. [*now accepts the intervention and engages*]

**Supervisor:** You were afraid maybe that opening up your feelings would expose you to criticism or ridicule? [*models reflection of feelings*]

**Supervisee:** Absolutely. I never felt that I had the luxury the White students had to cry in public or in class or to appear to "not know" what was going on. I pride myself on looking like I know what was going on. So I've never given myself permission to express or discuss feelings. I couldn't afford it. [*feels heard and engages more fully*]

**Supervisor:** And here I am, a White supervisor, so if we go together, or you go with your White client into the realm of feelings, it brings up those old feelings and fears.

**Supervisee:** Yep.

### Exploration of Feelings

**Supervisor:** I'm realizing that you just revealed the feeling of fear to me and the concerns behind that feeling. How does it feel to do that right now? [*models further focus on feeling*]

**Supervisee:** It's weird ... and pretty scary.

### Focus on the Supervisory Working Alliance

**Supervisor:** You're concerned that I might judge you for doing the very thing I'm asking you to do ...? What an awful bind to be in, Tasha. I'm so sad that being in this culture has made you feel like that. I'm even sadder that you may feel like that with me, too. [*brings the conversation back to the alliance*]

**Supervisee:** It's okay. I actually feel pretty okay with you. [*indicates trust*]

**Supervisor:** You had said it felt scary, so I wasn't sure.

**Supervisee:** Well, I mean it's scary in a general sense but not so much with you. I trust you. [*reflects on the general quality of the alliance, that it is rooted in trust*]

**Supervisor:** So how did it feel to have me label your feelings just now? [*explores feelings in the here and now*]

**Supervisee:** It felt really good, like you were open to me and understanding me. [*acknowledges benefit from having her feelings reflected*]

### Focus on Skill

**Supervisor:** Can you see how that kind of labeling might benefit a client? [*tries to evaluate the effect of the intervention*]

**Supervisee:** Yes I can now. But how do I do that like you did it?

**Supervisor:** Well, let's start right here. How do you think *I'm* feeling right now? [*invites supervisee to practice the skill*]

**Supervisee:** I think you are feeling pretty relieved that I just got your point. (*laughs*)

**Supervisor:** That was AWESOME! You are exactly right. That didn't seem so hard now, did it? [*validates supervisee's success in demonstrating the desired skill*]

**Supervisee:** Not really. (*laughs*) [*recognizes her own capacity to reflect feelings*]

**Supervisor:** It seems like you had the feeling right on the tip of your mind but this time you gave yourself permission to say it. Do you think you can practice more of giving yourself permission to do that with your clients? [*further validates the supervisee and recommends practice*]

**Supervisee:** I can try.

## Resolution

**Supervisor:** Good. Let's see how you do with it this week, okay? We know you *can* do it. [*acknowledges the supervisee's capacity, which has just been demonstrated*]

**Supervisee:** Okay . . . it's going to take some work and focus. [*commits to working on the skill*]

**Supervisor:** And breathing through it. [*provides support*]

**Supervisee:** And breathing through it.

In this interaction the supervisor models the very skill the supervisee needs to develop to illustrate its value for the supervisee. That is, the supervisor acknowledges the supervisee's struggles as an African American and related fear of negative evaluation from a White supervisor until the supervisee feels understood. Addressing the supervisee's fear within the context of the supervision relationship deepens the interaction and allows the supervisee to express her feelings in a safe interpersonal context. The supervisor then invites the supervisee to label the supervisor's feelings, which the supervisee does successfully. The supervisor endorses the supervisee's ability to reflect the supervisor's feelings and invites her to try it more with clients.

# ADDRESSING PROBLEMATIC EMOTIONS, ATTITUDES, AND BEHAVIORS

Skill difficulties and deficits are but one aspect of supervisee competency that must be addressed in supervision; there are other competency concerns that can interfere with the normal progression of a therapist's professional development. In 1999, authors Forrest, Elman, Gizara, and Vacha-Haase distinguished between incompetence and impaired performance in therapist development. They used the term *impaired* to describe a supervisee who had once exhibited competence but who encountered circumstances that interfered with his or her ability to demonstrate competence, whereas *incompetent* refers to the state of never having developed competence. In the course of working with supervisees, supervisors encounter supervisees who are impaired as well as supervisees who cannot establish competency. Given the conflation of the terms *impaired* and *disabled* we avoid the use of the term *impaired* to describe problematic supervisee behavior. Instead, we use the term *problematic*.

## Crisis in Confidence

Critical incidents related to competence are among the dilemmas most frequently discussed in supervision (Chen & Bernstein, 2000), particularly with novices (Rabinowitz, Heppner, & Roehlke, 1986). According to Hogan (1964), crises in confidence are common in therapists who have established initial relationships with their clients but are still unsure about how to manage the complexity of therapeutic intervention. Indeed, Mallinckrodt and Nelson (1991) found that students in their second practicum rated their working alliances with their clients significantly lower than they did when they were in their first practicum. These authors concluded that this discrepancy represented a normal and expected drop in confidence as supervisees began to recognize the realities and complexities of therapeutic intervention.

Because crises in confidence usually reflect temporary difficulties rather than incompetence, supervision typically involves normalizing supervisees' feelings about being overwhelmed and helping them develop therapeutic strategies to help them manage their cases. Often a client's improvement can remedy a temporary loss of confidence in the supervisee. Occasionally, however, a supervisee may have a client who is simply not going to improve. This is particularly the case when a client has a chronic mental illness that is resistant to both medical and psychotherapeutic interventions. Supervisees who are exposed to severe pathology in their clients can become discouraged and begin to doubt their abilities. Supervision in this kind of situation involves assisting the supervisee to recognize the limits of therapy effectiveness and not to take such situations personally. However, because developing therapists do need success experiences, it is important that supervisors work to ensure that their supervisees, particularly novices, are assigned cases in which they can feel effective. It is also important for supervisors to identify and acknowledge supervisee success with all clients, regardless of the magnitude of the success.

## Interpersonal and Characterological Difficulties

Whereas work-related stressors (crises in confidence, emotional exhaustion, and vicarious traumatization) result in problematic thoughts and feelings, supervisees with ongoing interpersonal and characterological difficulties come to their supervisors' attention because of problematic attitudes and challenging interpersonal behaviors. Although many psychotherapists enter the field with "baggage" related to trauma and thwarted needs in their personal histories (Barnett, 2007), problems arise when therapists, unaware of their unconscious needs and motivations, act inappropriately with clients, peers, and supervisors.

The aim of training in the psychoanalytic field is to help supervisees become aware of unconscious experiences so they can be understood, used, and managed as therapists work with clients. However, in many training settings, this type of insight is not the goal. Whether or not a supervisee is prompted to explore painful formative experiences, the outcomes of these early relationships can exercise a powerful influence on professional relationships. Moreover, attitudes learned in formative settings can negatively affect how therapists in training relate to others. For instance, a therapist who has been shaped to believe that every question has a right or wrong answer may have difficulty negotiating the ambiguity and complexity of most clients' difficulties. The defining elements in serious difficulties with a supervisee are the supervisee's resistance to understanding or his her impact on others, including clients, and an unwillingness to change.

## Process Model: Addressing Problematic Attitudes and Behavior

### Marker

Supervisees with serious characterological difficulties are unlikely to discuss them or easily accept their validity or importance. Furthermore, because characterological problems vary in intensity, the markers of a problematic attitude or behavior critical event are more difficult to decipher. A supervisee with entrenched personality difficulties may become extraordinarily uncooperative or hostile, may triangulate and "split" various supervisors and advisors by complaining vociferously to one about the other, or withdraw precipitously from the supervisory relationship. Markers may also become evident in group supervision, staff meetings, or the broader professional setting (e.g., with support staff, clients in the waiting room, or peers in common areas).

Of course, characterological difficulties also may surface in a supervisee's work with clients. Indeed, because people with serious relational problems often do not recognize these difficulties in themselves, markers can be signaled only by observation. For this reason, observations across situations (i.e., in therapy, in supervision, with peers, or in classes and seminars) are essential. In the absence of consistency across situations, it would be unwise to assume that a supervisee's lack of sensitivity with clients signals a characterological problem rather than an interpersonal or therapeutic skills deficit.

One common marker of characterological difficulties is a supervisor's excessive worry about a supervisee. Moreover, such worries and related consultations, extra supervision meetings, extra observations, and additional evaluations may take up an inordinate amount of a supervisor's time. The supervisor may become gradually more preoccupied with the realization that something about the supervisee's interactions with others is not healthy or functional. Sometimes the supervisor may feel consistently reactive to a particular supervisee's behavior in a way that is not familiar to the supervisor or mirrors the supervisor's reactions to clients and/or to supervisees who have been identified as having characterological problems. In extreme cases, supervisors may respond in ways that surprise themselves, such as with sudden anger, confusion, defensiveness, exasperation, or feelings of inadequacy around the supervisee. Distinguishing between a supervisee's profound skill deficiency and a serious personality disorder that will make it necessary to "counsel" a supervisee out of the profession is a particularly difficult challenge. It is possible that what looks like a personality disorder may be a stubborn interpersonal style that is actually amenable to change given proper intervention.

## Task Environment and Resolution

The task in these kinds of events is to address (not change) the supervisee's problematic behaviors, attitudes, and feelings. It is important to distinguish between skill difficulties and skill deficits, but it is also important to distinguish between a crisis in confidence or something more serious (e.g., vicarious traumatization). If the supervisee is simply having a crisis in confidence, a simple exploration of feelings and attending to the supervisee's needs may be all that is necessary. Listening carefully to the supervisee to uncover the source if his or her distress is critical, and allowing him or her to vent or process frustrations and stressors related to dealing with clients may result in improvement.

Focus on the supervisory alliance is also critical. In many situations involving challenging supervisee behaviors, an alliance rupture (Friedlander, 2015; Nelson, Gray, Friedlander, Ladany, & Walker, 2001) may have taken place. A rupture is defined as the outcome of a misunderstanding or conflict between supervisor and supervisee that has been left unaddressed and unresolved. In a rupture situation both parties experience discomfort in their interaction, and either or both may be unaware of the source of the discomfort. Regardless of whether a supervisor clearly understands the precipitant of the relational discomfort, it is important to address and process the discomfort. The discomfort may be a carry-over from an event in the therapy relationship, necessitating that the supervisor focus on the therapeutic process and attend to parallel process. Often a frank discussion of the source of conflict can diffuse the interpersonal distress and clarify what one or both parties need to do to avoid future misunderstandings.

Regardless of the cause of a challenging supervisee's behaviors, the supervisor must also evaluate her or his knowledge and skill. Thus, sequences involving assessing knowledge, focus on evaluation, and focus on skill may be important to a successful resolution of a problematic behavior event (see Figure 3.2 for addressing a prototypical event of this kind).

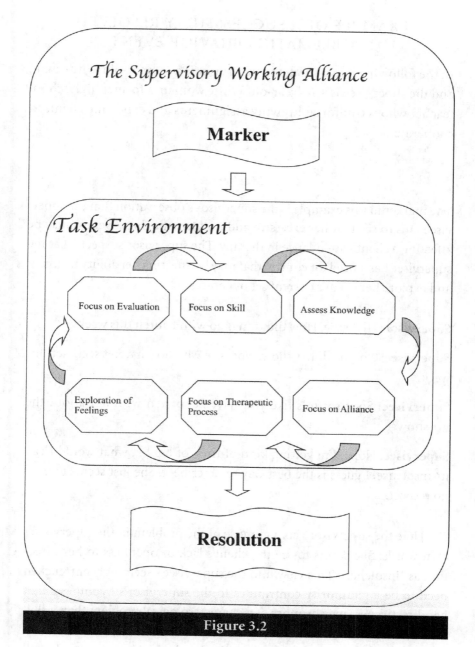

**Figure 3.2**

Process model for addressing a problematic supervisee behavior event.

## EXAMPLE OF A SUCCESSFULLY RESOLVED
## PROBLEMATIC BEHAVIOR EVENT

In the following interaction, the supervisor is a 45-year-old White man, and the supervisee is a 40-year-old White woman, a former high school teacher who is comfortable giving assignments and expecting clients to cooperate.

### Marker

The marker in this example is the supervisor's observation that the supervisee fails to see that her excessive and problematic directiveness may be affecting a client's attendance in therapy. The supervisor suspects that the supervisee has a need for control that may be affecting her ability to accept and explore her client's current set of choices.

**Supervisor:** Hi, Leslie. How did things go with Lauren this week?

**Supervisee:** Oh, she didn't show. Not sure why. So I haven't seen her this week.

**Supervisee:** So it sounds like you haven't spoken with her about the no-show?

**Supervisee:** Nope. I'm getting kind of tired of her . . . what would I call it? Insolence, I guess is the best way to describe it. She just seems to have no respect.

Here the supervisor gets a glimpse of the problem in the supervisee's own words. She seems to see the client's lack of openness to her direction as "insolence." This view into the supervisee's seemingly entrenched need to be an authority contributes to the supervisor's hypothesis that her directiveness may be more of a characterological problem than a skill deficit. He decides to test his hypothesis by offering the supervisee a direct suggestion. If she responds positively, he may be looking at a simple skill deficit. If she resists, he may be looking at a characterological issue.

## Task Environment

### Focus on Skill

**Supervisor:** I know she has been challenging for you, but I think it would be good to make contact and find out why she didn't come in. Okay? [*assumes a directive stance yet checks in with the supervisee*]

**Supervisee:** I mean, she comes in and sits and just looks at me defiantly. She gives one-word answers to my questions. It feels like she is a nonclient, so I'm not surprised she didn't come in. I wouldn't be surprised if she didn't come back at all.

**Supervisor:** Still, I think it would be a good idea to . . . [*maintains a directive stance*]

Here the supervisor as tried direction twice to influence the supervisee (to no avail). The focus on skill continues.

**Supervisee:** (*interrupts*) I know that she has a bad history, but that's no excuse for not participating in the very thing you have asked for. I know what she needs and that is to break up with this guy who has no job, who sits around the house all day playing video games while she goes to work and takes classes. When I ask her why she stays, she refuses to answer me. It's like, "Look, girlfriend, I am trying to help you here, and you are not participating. What do you want from me?" I get so exasperated. [*responds defensively*]

The supervisee's response to the supervisor's intervention confirms his hunch that he is dealing with her personality pattern rather than a skill deficit. In the following section, he pursues exploring the problem in greater depth.

### Exploration of Feelings

**Supervisor:** It's just so frustrating that she won't accept your guidance. [*recognizing the supervisee's resistance to focusing on her skills, shifts to explore her feelings in relation to the client's resistance*]

**Supervisee:** I told her last time we met that being a client means talking. I also told her that she needs to realize that she is making her own bed by staying with this guy and that she is depressed because she won't pull herself up. Being a client means you have got to be willing to change, and she isn't willing to change OR to be a client. So I've had it with her.

**Supervisor:** You feel like you want to fire her. [*reflects the supervisee's feelings of frustration*]

**Supervisee:** Yes. I absolutely do. It has been 3 years for her with this guy, and he hasn't worked since he quit taking the community college classes. And their rent is way too high. I can't believe she signed up to pay so much when she doesn't make enough to support both of them. She should have known he'd be a freeloader. So she is making some very bad decisions. And I have asked her what she thinks about her decision making, whether she thinks she makes good decisions, and she says yes. (*throws up her hands*) How can someone be that clueless? I told her that her decisions have gotten her into this mess, but she just won't listen. And she won't talk. So what am I supposed to do when a client won't be a client? [*vents further frustration*]

**Supervisor:** It's beginning to sound like you think she should behave the way you want her to and the fact that she won't take your advice leaves you feeling very stuck. [*reflects the source of the supervisee's frustration, demonstrating understanding of her feelings*]

**Supervisee:** Exactly!

### Assessing Knowledge

**Supervisor:** I know we've spoken before about your guiding theory or theories, and I'm wondering what theory is guiding you in your work with her. [*seeks to understand how the supervisee is conceptualizing her approach to the client*]

**Supervisee:** Well, my main theory is solution focused but I'm also wanting to use some CBT with clients, so I think eventually my theory will combine the two.

**Supervisor:** So it's important to you that clients make plans to change what they are doing so that they can reach their goals. [*personalizes the supervisee's meaning*]

**Supervisee:** Yes, and she won't. She sits and looks at me and won't engage in doing what is clearly in her best interest.

**Supervisor:** And that is . . . leaving the boyfriend? [*clarifies*]

**Supervisee:** Yes. (*looks expectantly at the supervisor*)

**Supervisor:** That sure seems like your goal . . . but it doesn't seem like *her* goal. [*tests to see how well supervisee really understands solution-focused therapy*]

**Supervisee:** Yes but it *should* be her goal! (*laughing and throwing up her hands*)

### Focus on the Therapeutic Process

**Supervisor:** You know, one of the key aspects of solution-focused therapy is that the client needs to be the one who identifies the goal or goals for counseling. Another key aspect is that the therapeutic alliance must be strong before goal setting can be successful. (*teaching*) So I'm wondering how you feel about the strength of your relationship with her. [*focuses on the supervisee's experience of her alliance with the client*]

**Supervisee:** Isn't that obvious? Her insolence is preventing us from having a very good relationship. Furthermore, I don't see how she can have good relationships with people in general with an attitude like that. She acts like a defiant child, and I am definitely not in the mood to work with defiant children. I have had two of my own (*laughing*) and that is enough. Plus I was a teacher for 14 years. I went back to school to get *away* from defiant children! (*still laughing*) I know very well what it is like to have to face someone down, and I can do it, but I didn't come here because I wanted to have to keep doing it. I came here to learn to work with people who *want* to change. [*has a simplistic understanding of her relationship to the client, with little awareness of how her interpersonal style may be affecting the client*]

### Focus on Skill

**Supervisor:** You know, a lot of people come to therapy because they want help but it turns out they may not be ready to change, not yet anyway. [*teaches*]

**Supervisee:** Sorry, but I don't buy that. You don't come to therapy and pay someone unless you want to change or unless you are looking for a fight and you are willing to pay for it. I think this client is looking for a fight. It sounded like she always fought with her mother, and now she fights constantly with her boyfriend. I don't think she should come into therapy wanting to fight with me, but it seems like she does sometimes. She is just so exasperating. Did I tell you that last session she sat for like 10 minutes without saying *anything*? Is that the way to treat your therapist? [*actively resists the supervisor's intervention*]

**Supervisor:** So she's used to being in conflict, and now she's in conflict with you. [*reflects, trying to model understanding*]

**Supervisee:** I suppose so, but you'd think she'd have some respect, you know? I mean I am not her mother, God forbid, though I'm almost old enough to be. She needs to learn to have some respect. I get very impatient when younger people don't show respect. I was quite strict with my students when I taught high school, which is why I was let go. I don't know how these young principals get the idea you should allow your students to chew gum in class. I am glad they let me go anyway so I could make a career change. But anyway, I don't see how these young clients think they can get away with being so defiant in therapy. I thought doing therapy would be different. (*tears up*)

### Exploration of Feelings

**Supervisor:** Seems like it's really, really hard for you not to feel respected. [*reflects*]

**Supervisee:** Yes. (*cries softly*) Yes. God, I'm sorry. I should be on task. (*grabs a tissue*)

**Supervisor:** We *are* on task, Leslie. (*gently*)

**Supervisee:** No we aren't! We should be talking about my clients.

**Supervisor:** We are talking about your feelings about your client and how it hurts you so much that she won't be the kind of client you had hoped you'd be seeing.

**Supervisee:** God, I hope there aren't many of *her* out there. Maybe I should talk about one of my other clients today. Sorry I am not doing what I'm supposed to do in supervision. [*begins to recognize a strain with the supervisor*]

### Focus on the Supervisory Alliance

**Supervisor:** You are being who you are right now, here with me, with your intense disappointment, and this is *just* what we should be doing here. [*validates supervisee's behavior*]

**Supervisee:** Hey, I don't need counseling. I'm sorry.

**Supervisor:** Have you ever had counseling?

**Supervisee:** No. I haven't really needed it. I am tough, always had to be, which is why this is so embarrassing. (*grabs another tissue*).

**Supervisor:** I really appreciate your willingness to be genuine right now. (*moment of silence*) [*reflects on the here and now, validating the supervisee's behavior*]

**Supervisee:** This feels so strange and really embarrassing. [*recognizes that intimacy in the here and now is a new and uncomfortable experience for her*]

**Supervisor:** Something tells me that this is a new feeling—that you have permission to just let down and be with your feelings of helplessness and disappointment, as well as the discomfort that comes from sharing these feelings with me. [*reflects feelings and meaning*]

**Supervisee:** I am not supposed to (a) have these feelings and (b) embarrass myself and you by exhibiting them in here.

**Supervisor:** So as much as I'd like you to hear that it is okay for you to have your feelings right now, you aren't comfortable hearing me say that. [*wonders if the supervisee can take an observer perspective*]

**Supervisee:** No. I am not.

**Supervisor:** Okay. That's okay. [*demonstrates acceptance of the supervisee's need to not be pushed, hoping to model acceptance*]

(*another moment of silence*)

**Supervisee:** (*more tears*)

**Supervisor:** Yeah. Lots of stuff there. Mmhmm. [*reiterates permission to be in the moment*]

**Supervisee:** Yeah. (*finishes crying*)

### Exploration of Feelings

**Supervisor:** What's going on for you now? [*inquires about here-and-now experience, modeling responsiveness*]

**Supervisee:** I'm not sure. This is a new feeling, kind of relief. I feel like I have failed some kind of test . . . but I feel better.

**Supervisor:** What kind of test have you failed? [*elicits supervisee's self-observation*]

**Supervisee:** I'm supposed to be composed and professional at all times.

### Focus on the Supervisory Alliance

**Supervisor:** That's an awfully tall order. [*challenges supervisee's negative self-assessment*]

**Supervisee:** Yeah, but this is a professional setting, and I should be professional here. I didn't mean to disrespect you. [*attempts to repair the relationship that she feels she has damaged*]

**Supervisor:** I just experienced you being *very* professional, and I did not feel disrespected. You bravely owned your feelings of disappointment and had the courage to express them fully with me. As therapists working together, that is a very sophisticated kind of professionalism. [*normalizes the supervisee's expression of feelings and reframes her behavior as productive*]

**Supervisee:** That is so different.

**Supervisor:** What do you think enabled you to do that? You were so sure you didn't want to let down. [*leaves the discussion open to focus on supervisee experience of supervisory relationship*]

**Supervisee:** I was just so upset, I'm not sure I could help it. But you told me it was okay to do it or not to do it. That was strange. It was like I could choose without seeming to be disrespectful. [*focuses on supervisory relationship*]

**Supervisor:** So seems like you needed and on some level wanted to feel like you could be the one to decide what to do. "It was going to be okay with me either way?" [*reflects*]

**Supervisee:** Yeah. That is so strange.

**Supervisor:** How is it strange? [*models how to draw out a feeling*]

**Supervisee:** To feel like whatever I decide is okay and that we're good no matter what I decide. If I didn't do what my mother expected—always—I was told I was being disrespectful.

**Supervisor:** So in your experience there is typically a right way and a wrong way to go about things and if you didn't do as you were told, you came to believe that was being disrespectful. Here you were able to just go with what you needed rather than try to do the "right" thing. [*validates supervisee's right to express a need, concomitantly illustrating the nature of the problematic dichotomous thinking*]

### Attend to Parallel Process

**Supervisee:** Yeah. It felt so different to be able to choose. I wonder if I need to do that for my client, just not expect her to solve her problems the way I think she should. [*demonstrates an awareness of the parallel process and a change in her understanding of the therapeutic process*]

**Supervisor:** Yes, it's funny how that parallel works.

### Focus on Skill and Focus on the Therapeutic Process

**Supervisor:** How would you communicate to her that you don't have that expectation? [*brings the focus back to a therapy skill*]

**Supervisee:** First, I would stop asking her why she stays with the boyfriend, as if I think she is getting it wrong. I think I communicate some exasperation to her when she comes back and complains about something he has done. Maybe I need to just let her have her feelings for a while.

**Supervisor:** How will you demonstrate that you are willing to let her have her feelings? [*invites supervisee to operationalize her intent*]

**Supervisee:** I suppose just be with her when she talks about them.

**Supervisor:** Maybe empathize, label the feelings. [*makes a suggestion*]

**Supervisee:** . . . label them, yeah. Be with her in them. [*indicates acceptance of the suggestion*]

**Supervisor:** Let her decide what to do?

**Supervisee:** Yeah. I wonder if she will decide on her own.

**Supervisor:** Could be. Sounds like you think it's worth a try. [*allows supervisee to own the impetus for change, hoping the supervisee will do the same for the client*]

**Supervisee:** Yeah.

## Focus on Evaluation

**Supervisor:** It seems like this business about having to do the right thing or risk being disrespectful has been an ongoing issue for you for a long time, and I have some concern that it may continue to dog you in your future work. [*reviews supervisee issues and expresses concern about their potential ongoing challenge for the supervisee*]

**Supervisee:** It has, forever. Do you think I need therapy? [*expresses receptiveness to change*]

**Supervisor:** I think it would make your development as a therapist a heck of a lot easier, Leslie, and that you'd become much more skilled as a result of seeing what it's like on the other side.

**Supervisee:** Oh Lord, this upsets my whole apple cart.

**Supervisor:** Maybe with some therapy you will find that there aren't as many rotten apples in there as you thought there were. [*validating the supervisee's personhood*]

**Supervisee:** (*laughing*) Maybe so.

## Resolution

**Supervisor:** Would you like me to give you a couple of names of therapists I think you would feel safe talking to about this?

**Supervisee:** Sure. If it can help me succeed, I'll do it.

**Supervisor:** I think it has the potential to help you develop as a therapist and as a person.

**Supervisee:** Thank you. This has been a hard conversation for me and probably for you too.

**Supervisor:** Hard but worth it, I hope. What about this conversation has been useful?

**Supervisee:** I suppose I need to learn to give my clients more room to decide things on their own. I guess I may have a need to be in charge that doesn't work so well in therapy, and I probably need to explore that. That tendency got me in trouble when I was teaching, too. I think I should talk to someone about it. I didn't see it quite this clearly before. So thanks.

**Supervisor:** You are quite welcome, Leslie. Do you think you can call your client now and see if she's coming back?

**Supervisee:** Okay. I'll do that now. Should I ask her if I did something to make her feel uncomfortable talking to me? Oh, God, that would be so hard. [*initiates an intervention idea, asking if it would be the "right" thing*]

**Supervisor:** What do YOU think? [*returns the "decision ball" to the supervisee's court*]

**Supervisee:** I think I should.

**Supervisor:** (*smiling*) Good for you! [*expresses confidence in the supervisee's judgment*]

Early in this interaction, the supervisor feels some exasperation with his supervisee regarding the rigid role expectations she has for her clients and herself. As Leslie begins to rant about her client, the supervisor is uncertain about whether Leslie's character structure is so rigid that she will be unable to benefit from supervision. The supervisor makes a strategic decision to use the supervisory process to model responsiveness (cf. Friedlander, 2012, 2015), thereby showing the supervisee how to provide a facilitative clinical context within which a client feels permission to be open about feelings and choose a course of action.

This supervisory task is successfully resolved and the supervisee's character structure is shown to be not as rigid as the supervisor initially feared. In "real life," of course, this process model might actually take longer than it does in this vignette. It might require most of a session or continue throughout two or more sessions. The length of the process ultimately depends on the ability of the supervisee to receive it and respond to it. Regardless of length, supervisors should return to what their supervisee has learned about interpersonal process and how that may apply to her or his work with a particular client or clients in general—the focus eventually returning to a better understanding of the therapeutic process and thus skill development to facilitate that process.

Near the end of the above scenario is the endorsement of the notion of seeking personal psychotherapy. Referral of a supervisee for psychotherapy is a common practice, and personal therapy for developing therapists is valued throughout the profession. In cases in which serious impairment is determined, therapy may be one condition of training probation.

## SPECIAL CONSIDERATIONS: COUNSELING "IN" AND "OUT"

There are numerous creative approaches to help a supervisee improve his or her performance, including additional clinical coursework, intensified supervision, greater direct observation and consultation, and personal psychotherapy. Assisting a supervisee to undertake remedial procedures may be considered a "counseling in" process aimed at retaining the supervisee in his or her program or placement.

Although supervisors have a duty to provide creative opportunities for supervisees to change and grow, supervisors' responsibility to protect the welfare of current and future clients is paramount. Over time a supervisor and/or training program may conclude that a supervisee's interpersonal difficulties are characterological in nature and beyond remediation. Because counseling and therapy are grounded in the process of personal and interpersonal change and because supervisee's intractable interpersonal patterns have the potential to harm clients, it may be necessary to advise the student to discontinue her or his mental health training. "Counseling out" should be as supportive a process as possible, assisting a supervisee to recognize that the demands of the profession are not a good fit for her or him. The process should include a frank discussion of the supervisee's limitations and the failure of remediation attempts to alter those limitations, along with active encouragement of the supervisee's exploration of other potential career paths.

The process of counseling a supervisee out of the profession is a last resort, a gatekeeping measure built into the training process to ensure the protection of the public. In the interest of informed consent (see *Guidelines for Clinical Supervision in Health Service Psychology*, American Psychological Association [APA], 2014), supervisees should be fully aware at the outset of their training that should they encounter obstacles in the training process, they are afforded due process, or the right to a "fair hearing." Due process in psychotherapy training is a structured set of remedies that are built into the training process should obstacles occur.

Training sites and academic programs should provide supervisees with informed consent documents that outline program or agency expectations, timing and type of evaluations, and the extent to which supervisees are allowed to respond to evaluations (APA, 2014). These documents should provide definitions of inadequate progress toward specific competencies and details about the remediation process. The documents should clarify that procedures will be followed in the case of inadequate progress or problematic behavior. Due process documents also describe in detail procedures for addressing supervisee grievances. In the case of prelicensure supervision in a private practice, due process definitions and procedures can be detailed in the supervisory contract. Forrest et al. (1999)

provided a thorough examination of problematic supervisee attitudes and behavior, as well as the procedures that informed the creation of due process documents in clinical training programs across the United States. The provision of due process information to supervisees at the outset of their supervision experience protects everyone, including the training program, the supervisor, the supervisee, and the clients.

# CONCLUSION

Learning to be a professional therapist is a daunting task, the enormity of which may be lost on novice and early-career supervisees. Encountering one's lack of skill or awareness in the process of becoming a therapist can be frightening and often threatening for supervisees. Supervisors are key to assisting supervisees to accept their current state of development and commit to further learning. Whether a supervisor is concerned about simple skill difficulties, skill deficiencies, crises in confidence, vicarious traumatization, or problematic attitudes behaviors, the supervisory relationship is an important vehicle for promoting supervisee understanding, growth, and even healing. Some of the critical interpersonal supervision sequences described in this section included exploration of feelings, attend to parallel process, and focus on the supervisory alliance, interventions that might not be included in every supervisor's compendium of approaches. However, we believe that this interpersonal stance can create pivotal experiences for supervisees that can be both instructional and motivating.

# 4

# Working Through Parallel Processes and Heightening Multicultural Awareness: Two Critical Events for the Price of One

As we mentioned in Chapter 1, critical events do not necessarily occur in a linear fashion, such that a new event waits for a previous event to finish. Rather, events often overlap and can intertwine with other events. To illustrate this phenomenon, we use this chapter to discuss a new, previously unpublished critical event, working through parallel processes, and illustrate its overlap and link with a multicultural awareness event, an event that interested readers can find more fully addressed in Ladany, Friedlander, and Nelson (2005).

Before moving forward, we need to distinguish a supervisor's focus on parallel process as an interactional sequence in our model and working through parallel processes as the task in a parallel process event. As shown later in this chapter, attend to parallel process is a salient interactional sequence, which we define as a "discussion that draws attention to similarities between a specific therapeutic interaction and the supervisory

http://dx.doi.org/10.1037/14916-005
*Supervision Essentials for the Critical Events in Psychotherapy Supervision Model*, by N. Ladany, M. L. Friedlander, and M. L. Nelson

interaction. Parallel processes may originate in either interaction and be mirrored in the other." A parallel process event consists of multiple interactional sequences, including of course, attend to parallel process. We discuss these distinctions in the case examples later in the chapter.

We begin the chapter with an overview of the literature on parallel process. We then provide a process model for working through a parallel process event, followed by an illustrative case. We then review a heightening multicultural awareness event and demonstrate how it can overlap with a parallel process event. We offer this illustration because critical events often overlap (i.e., a new event often does not occur only after another event is resolved).

Searles (1955) first described a supervisory situation whereby the supervisor may be having supervisor countertransference reactions coming from the therapy relationship. He referred to this concept as the reflection process. Building on Searles' formulation, Ekstein and Wallerstein (1958, 1972) identified a phenomenon that they called parallel process (p. 177), whereby similar transference-countertransference processes were occurring in therapy and supervision. In addition, these authors noted that the parallels could be coming upward from the therapy relationship or downward from the supervisory relationship. In time, other authors built upon the constructs (e.g., Friedlander, Siegel, & Brenock, 1989; Gross Doehrman, 1976; Ladany, Walker, Pate-Carolan, & Gray Evans, 2008; Mothersole, 1999; Sripada, 1999; Tracey, Bludworth, & Glidden-Tracey, 2012; Walker, 2003).

In relation to our critical events model, we define parallel processes as dyadic reactions that occur in supervision that mirror dyadic reactions in psychotherapy (or vice versa) and are meaningful for supervisee learning. Reactions consist of thoughts, feelings, and behaviors on the part of the supervisor, therapist, and client(s) about which each participant may have varying degrees of awareness. Parallel processes can be initiated in therapy and transferred to supervision or vice versa. In addition, the bidirectional parallel processes can be proximal in that they occur in the subsequent supervision or therapy session, or distal in that they occur after multiple supervision or therapy sessions. Finally, as we define it, parallel processes can be worked through when the supervisor facilitates a corrective relational experience for the supervisee, as explained later.

Parallel processes should be distinguished from general processes that appear similar in therapy and supervision. In other words, parallel processes should be meaningful and illustrative of challenges that are occurring in supervision and/or therapy. For example, the fact that both supervisors and supervisees, like therapists and clients, talk with one another does not mean that "talking" is a parallel process because the simple act of talking lacks specific meaning in either context. In a similar vein, a situation in which a supervisee working with an anxious client presents as anxious in her supervision session is not necessarily indicative of a clinically meaningful parallel process. A supervisee's high anxiety may simply be characteristic of the individual. However, in as much as the supervisee's anxiety is based on or triggered by the client's anxiety, a parallel process has occurred. It is up to the supervisor to help the supervisee distinguish the clinical meaningfulness of the identified parallel process.

Research on parallel process has largely been conducted using case studies (Alpher, 1991; Friedlander et al., 1989; Grant, Schofield, & Crawford, 2012; Gross Doehrman, 1976; Jacobsen, 2007; Ladany & Inman, 2012; Ladany et al., 2008). The phenomenon has also been examined through surveys (Raichelson, Herron, Primavera, & Ramirez, 1997) and sophisticated quantitative models (Tracey et al., 2012). Across these investigations, parallel processes, which early authors considered to be unconscious, have been observed, and the phenomenon seems to be meaningful for supervisors across theoretical orientations.

For parallel process events to be meaningful, supervisors need to be open to identifying and examining the phenomenon. Supervisees whose supervisors are unaware, unconvinced, or unwilling to consider parallel processes are likely to lose out on the learning opportunities and clinical benefits provided by an understanding of parallel processes. Even if supervisors are skeptical of the unconscious basis for parallel process, consider that supervisees are in a one-down position in supervision but a one-up position in their therapy relationships (Friedlander, 2015; Friedlander et al., 1989; Tracey et al., 2012). These opposing relational positions (i.e., submissiveness versus dominance) can result in a mirroring effect on a behavioral level.

In the following section, we discuss a process model for assisting supervisees to work through parallel process reactions. We also illustrate two parallel process events, one that is unsuccessfully resolved and one that suggests a positive outcome.

## PROCESS MODEL: WORKING THROUGH PARALLEL PROCESSES

### Marker

Markers of parallel process events can originate from any member of the supervision or therapy dyad. The supervisor may notice that the supervisee is behaving in a manner that is uncharacteristic. For example, a supervisee may react to the supervisor in an unusually sarcastic fashion. Alternatively, in a particular supervision session, a supervisee may appear especially anxious, outside the range of her or his typical level of anxiety.

In both situations, the supervisor should ask about the presentation style of the supervisee's client to determine whether a parallel process may be occurring. Alternatively, the supervisor may be aware of a client's difficult interpersonal style and then reflect on whether the supervisee's behavior in supervision mirrors that style.

When supervisees are explicitly afforded the opportunity to consider the parallel process phenomenon as part of their role induction to supervision, the marker may be a direct comment about the possible occurrence of the phenomenon. In these cases, a supervisee may speculate about the possible occurrence of a parallel process, and the supervisor can follow up by initiating the task environment. Alternatively, a marker may come from a supervisor's self-reflection on his or her own reactions to the supervisee and whether these reactions are mirrored in the therapy relationship. For example, a supervisor may note that he is becoming overly directive during a supervision session but only recognizes his own uncharacteristic behavior after observing the supervisee's directiveness with her client.

## Task Environment and Resolution

After the identification of the marker, the task environment typically involves these interactional sequences: focus on the supervisory alliance, focus on the therapeutic process, exploration of feelings, attend to parallel process, and normalize experience. Compared to the task environments for other critical events, the interactional sequences may be more numerous in a parallel process event, essentially because multiple relationships are addressed. As shown in the following case example, additional sequences can be anticipated depending on the type of parallel process (e.g., focus on multicultural awareness).

By definition, a parallel process event requires a noticeable shift in the supervisory work: that is, the supervisor behaves responsively to the supervisee by changing the focus from a discussion of therapy to a discussion of what is occurring in supervision (Friedlander, 2012, 2015). For example, when a supervisee appears unusually tired or stressed, it behooves the supervisor to notice this change and "check in" about whether the supervisee's experience has something to do with what is occurring between them in supervision. Such inquiry is unlikely to prompt a role conflict if, as part of the supervision role induction and informed consent, the supervisee understands that supervision involves exploring his personal experience to disentangle and understand parallel processes. This check-in may simply involve asking the supervisee if processing more deeply what has occurred in his therapy relationships is acceptable before initiating the task environment of the event.

With at least a tacit agreement, the supervisor can move to the sequence focus on the therapeutic process. This sequence involves asking the supervisee about a particular client whom she may find challenging. From there the supervisor can inquire about her reactions to her client, particularly her affective reactions. Moreover, the supervisor could ask the supervisee to consider how her client may be feeling and reacting to what is occurring between them.

In the following example, the supervisor asks the supervisee to recall a previous session. However, a similar query could be used to explore the supervisee's reactions while observing a video recording of the therapy session during supervision session (e.g., a modified interpersonal process recall; Kagan [Klein], & Kagan, 1997).

Often it is the supervisor who recognizes the mirroring between therapy and supervision, but with experience, the supervisee may be the first one to notice the parallel process. In either situation, the supervisor attends to the parallel process by discussing the similar emotional reactions and/or behaviors that are occurring in both dyads.

Alternatively, the supervisor could facilitate a corrective relational experience with the supervisee that in turn is transmitted downward to the therapy work. In supervision, a corrective relational experience involves an intrapersonal shift in the supervisee's understanding of an event that is taking place in supervision (Ladany et al., 2012). For example, rather than respond to the supervisee's uncharacteristic and heightened anxiety by dismissing it as "just a bad day" or by focusing on a different issue altogether, the supervisor may ask the supervisee to explore the anxiety reaction further for the source and let the supervisee "sit with" the anxiety. It is possible, that in turn the supervisee would encourage her client to "sit with" heightened anxiety. Depending on the supervisee's experience with parallel processes, the supervisor may normalize the experience.

We have found that the identification of parallel processes is often accompanied by an *ah-ha* experience that can be at once pleasant and disorienting, particularly when the parallel process is outside the supervisee's awareness. The change in awareness and subsequent changes in the supervisee's approach to therapy are an integral part of the resolution of this critical event. The process model appears in Figure 4.1.

Of course, the prototypical example of a parallel process event is one in which a particular relational dynamic begins in the supervisee's therapy relationship and his corrective relational experience occurs subsequently in his relationship with the supervisor. Alternatively, the supervisor's behavior could initiate a corrective relational experience for the supervisee by an exploration of feelings, moving to a focus on the therapeutic process, and finally with the sequences attend to the parallel process and normalize the experience.

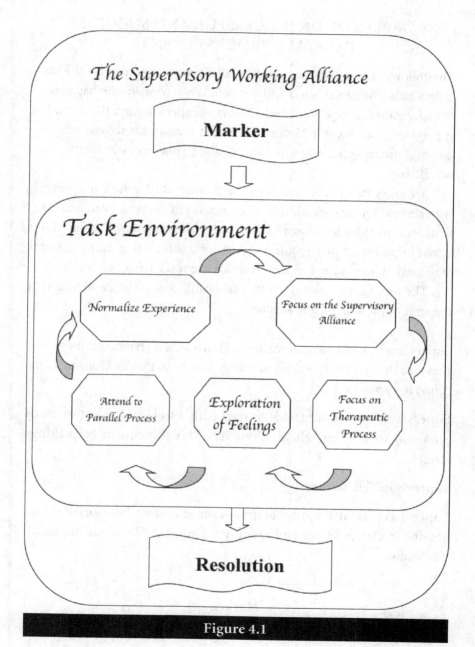

## Figure 4.1

Example of a parallel process event.

## EXAMPLES OF UNSUCCESSFUL AND SUCCESSFUL PARALLEL PROCESS EVENTS

The following case illustrates two parallel process events with the same individuals. The supervisor is a 40-year-old White woman who has 10 years of experience as a supervisor and 15 years of experience as a therapist. The supervisee, Arcadio, is a 25-year-old Latino man in his second year of a doctoral program. He has a physical disability that requires him to use a wheelchair.

Arcadio's two clients are Sylvia, a 28-year-old Latina who presents with generalized anxiety disorder (i.e., excessive worrying, headaches, difficulties at work), and Irene, a 45-year-old White woman with a significant visual impairment that requires the use of a service dog. Irene presents with anxiety after a car accident in which she was a passenger.

The setting is a community mental health clinic. The event begins at the start of the supervision session.

**Supervisor:** So, what would you like to learn today? [*typical opening question for this supervisor, who immediately focuses on the "task" aspect of the supervisory alliance*]

**Supervisee:** I'm not sure what to start with. I feel like I've got so much going on with all my clients these days. It's difficult to keep things straight.

**Supervisor:** Tell me more.

**Supervisee:** I think it's just that time of the semester where lots of things are due in classes. Paper and exam time, my client load has increased, you know.

### Marker

**Supervisor:** Sounds a bit overwhelming. [*notices that Arcadio's presentation is different from past supervision sessions, where he tended to be more even in his affect; leaves it open to see which direction he will take*]

92

**Supervisee:** Yeah, more than a bit! I'm also not sleeping well, worried about things. I used to do this occasionally but now it's affecting my sleep.

**Supervisor:** That is a lot. That doesn't sound like you. [*probes*]

**Supervisee:** It's not. I mean, at times this has happened in my life, but this past week leading up to our meeting has been rough.

**Supervisor:** Do you think there is anything about our meeting that may be triggering this for you? [*assesses whether his uncharacteristic behavior may be due to their past interactions*]

**Supervisee:** (*puzzled*) No, not that I can think of. I've always enjoyed coming here for supervision.

**Supervisor:** But something seems different . . . ? [*probes for a fuller description*]

**Supervisee:** I suppose.

At this point the supervisor considers that Arcadio's distorted (e.g., transferential) reaction is a marker of a parallel process event. The event moves next to the task environment.

## Task Environment

### Focus on the Supervisory Alliance

**Supervisor:** I appreciate your honesty. Perhaps we can step back a moment and consider how things are going in our supervision sessions. Sound okay? [*refocuses the work on the goals and tasks of the alliance, anticipating that the need to be particularly empathic moving forward*]

**Arcadio:** Sure.

**Supervisor:** Good. We began the session by my asking what you'd like to discuss today, and you followed up with talking about having lots going on, which led to us discussing how you having been feeling overwhelmed. Sound about right? [*clarifies, checking mutual perceptions*]

**Supervisee:** (*smiles*) Yeah. Captured perfectly!

**Supervisor:** I'm wondering if it's okay if we get specific about some of the overwhelming facets of your life, particularly in relation to your client load. [*negotiates an agreement on the session's tasks*]

**Supervisee:** That's fine. It's funny, when you call it a client "load," it sounds more than it is.

**Supervisor:** How so?

**Supervisee:** Well, I've only got four clients. One hasn't started, and one is finishing up. We've talked about the one finishing up in our past sessions, and I feel pretty good about how things went with him.

**Supervisor:** Then how about we talk about the other two? [*negotiates the task*]

### Focus on the Therapeutic Process

**Supervisee:** That works. First there's Irene, who was in a car accident a few weeks ago, and she is having PTSD reactions lately.

**Supervisor:** Like what?

**Supervisee:** She feels tense when she's in a car, hypervigilant and worried. She's reported bad nightmares. I'm not sure it's full-blown PTSD but certainly some of the key symptoms are there.

**Supervisor:** Was she driving the car when the accident occurred?

**Supervisee:** (*slightly smiles*) No. She's actually blind.

**Supervisor:** Oh, I didn't know.

**Supervisee:** When the accident happened she was most upset about her service dog, who fortunately was not injured in the accident. My second client is Sylvia, who's been having symptoms that include excessive worrying and headaches. It's affecting her work with what I think is generalized anxiety disorder.

At this point the supervisor, in a desire to help Arcadio, may have decided to provide him with informational resources on the treatment of generalized anxiety disorder (GAD), as well as recommend some approaches he could use in his session with Sylvia. In other words, the supervisor could take a didactic approach by directing Arcadio how to manage this case in hopes that this lengthy discussion would generalize to his work with other clients with GAD. However, with a focus on skills (conceptual, technical), the opportunity to help Arcadio use his inner experience with the client to inform his interventions would have been lost. Moreover, as shown later, the corrective relational experience would not have occurred. Thus, the parallel process event would not have been resolved successfully.

**Supervisor:** It sounds like you have done a nice job assessing and diagnosing both of your clients. Tell me more about what it's like to be in the therapy session. For example, when you're with Sylvia, what's happening?

**Supervisee:** Typically, she talks a lot about all of her worries. And she jumps from one topic to another. I can barely get a word in.

**Supervisor:** What's that like for you? [*realizes the need to be more specific*]

**Supervisee:** It's very frustrating. I have things I want to say, but I don't want to be rude and interrupt. And she keeps going on and on. First she talks about her boss, who she's having problems with. He doesn't seem to be treating her well. Then she'll jump to talking about her father, who has Alzheimer's and is in a nursing home. And how difficult he is to be around and how her sister won't help her take care of him. And this goes on to other topics. By the end of the session I'm all anxious and tense and feel as though we haven't gotten anywhere. Oh, she also spends a great deal of time talking about her worries about her kids.

As Arcadio is describing his client, the supervisor picks up on his anxious affect. She also recognizes a potential link between the client's emotional state and Arcadio's presentation. The moment Arcadio begins spinning out, similar to the client, is the same moment the supervisor decides to intervene by exploring Arcadio's feelings in the here and now, in hopes that this intervention will facilitate a successful resolution.

## Exploration of Feelings

**Supervisor:** Arcadio. Let me interrupt you a moment. I want you to try something, okay? [*by asking permission, the supervisor demonstrates how to attend to the alliance before moving forward*]

**Supervisee:** Okay.

**Supervisor:** How are you feeling right now?

**Supervisee:** Well, there's just so much that I feel I need to tell you about what she's presenting with. [*describes his thoughts, not his feelings*]

**Supervisor:** Hold on a moment. I want you to do me a favor and just sit with what you're experiencing. Don't say anything. Just let yourself feel whatever you are feeling right in the moment. [*models a here-and-now intervention that the supervisee can use with clients*]

**Supervisee:** Okay.

**Supervisor:** Good. Just be present with whatever feelings are coming up. (*long pause*) What are you feeling right now?

**Arcadio:** Anxious, nervous, a little scared.

**Supervisor:** Can you say more about these feelings?

**Supervisee:** It's weird, I'm not sure why I feel scared. Like something bad is going to happen. I know nothing bad will happen—intellectually. It's more a gut feeling. I need to remember the mindfulness work I've done.

**Supervisor:** How might that work right now?

**Supervisee:** Just breathe and be in the moment. Focus on my breathing.

**Supervisor:** Okay. That sounds good. Go ahead. [*models patience*]

**Supervisee:** (*briefly closes his eyes, exhales*) That's a little better.

**Supervisor:** Good. It sounds like the anxiety was taking over, and you've now found a way to counteract it and become more present. [*wants to be* *sure Arcadio has found a way to contain the anxiety before moving forward to raise the possibility of a parallel process]*

**Supervisee:** Definitely.

### Attend to Parallel Process

**Supervisor:** You know, Arcadio, I've noticed that today you seemed a little more anxious than you typically are in supervision. It was unique compared to our past supervision sessions. And at the same time you've mentioned a couple of clients who are rather anxious. Do you see any similarities in how they have presented to you in therapy and how you've felt today in supervision?

**Supervisee:** Definitely! Is this the "parallel process" that we talked about in class?

**Supervisor:** It seems so, at least to me. What's that like to identify it?

**Supervisee:** I'm a little taken aback. Now I feel a little . . . embarrassed. How could I have missed it?

Often supervisees who experience parallel processes for the first time are struck by how obvious it all is. The shift in thinking that accompanies this awareness is relieving but also embarrassing, particularly for supervisees who tend to perform well in general. Thus, it is important for supervisors to normalize the experience to enable it to be recognized in the future.

### Normalize the Experience

**Supervisor:** It's always a little disorienting to experience parallel process for the first time.

**Supervisee:** Wow, definitely.

**Supervisor:** And that's to be expected. The only way to learn about things sometimes is by experiencing them.

**Supervisee:** I suppose. It's also very exciting to see it firsthand.

**Supervisor:** Indeed. So what can be learned from this experience? [*wanting to help him translate this learning moment to actions he can use in his next therapy sessions*]

### Focus on the Therapeutic Process

**Supervisee:** Wow. It seems like a lot. First, I will be more patient with Sylvia.

**Supervisor:** How do you mean?

**Supervisee:** Maybe "patient" isn't what I mean. I'll be more likely to interrupt her, just the way you cut me off. And I really liked how you were with me in the moment. It helped me reflect on what I was actually feeling. [*demonstrates awareness of the parallel process*]

**Supervisor:** Do you think she will respond in a similar manner?

**Supervisee:** Probably not. She'll probably just run me over.

**Supervisor:** She may try. So unlike you, who is more likely to be able to sit with feelings in the moment, it may take more attempts with her.

**Supervisee:** Yeah, you're probably right. So I should just keep interrupting until she gets it?

**Supervisor:** What do you suppose? [*empowers him to think it through himself*]

**Supervisee:** Well, if I interrupt her too much, she may say enough of this and bolt.

**Supervisor:** Then you may have to lower your expectations of her ability to gain a similar level of insight in the same amount of time. [*directly instructs about responsiveness*]

**Supervisee:** Definitely.

## Resolution

**Supervisor:** Anything else left to discuss in relation to the parallel process? [*models responsiveness—how to "check in" with a client*]

**Arcadio:** I don't think so. This has helped a great deal.

**Supervisor:** Wonderful.

The event ended with what seemed to be a successful resolution. However, as noted later in this chapter, the resolution was only a partial one. That is, at the end of the session, the supervisor noted a "slight nagging" feeling but put it aside in the excitement about having successfully worked through a parallel process event. When we pick up this case again, it will become clear what her nagging feeling meant. However, first it is important to review another type of critical event: heightening multicultural awareness.

## HEIGHTENING MULTICULTURAL AWARENESS

The critical events model (Ladany et al., 2005) includes heightening multicultural awareness as an important task within supervision. Since the 2005 publication of our book, multicultural counseling and psychotherapy have received increased attention in the literature. However, there continues to be a dearth of new scholarship in this area of supervision (Ancis & Ladany, 2010; Ladany & Inman, 2012). For purposes of this chapter, we provide an overview of a multicultural critical event, with some updates based on the literature since 2005.

For our purposes, multicultural factors include age, gender, race, ethnicity, sexual orientation, ability status, social class, religion, and family structure, as well as the intersectionality of all these multicultural factors. In Ladany et al. (2005), we devoted one chapter to gender-based misunderstandings. To date, two studies examined gender-related events and their relation to supervisees' experiences of the supervisor (Bertsch et al., 2014; Walker et al., 2007). For case illustrations and detailed descriptions of gender-based critical events, see Ladany and Friedlander (2014) and Friedlander, Blanco, Bernardi, and Shaffer (in press). For purposes of the current chapter, we include gender as one multicultural factor among other sociocultural differences.

Supervisor multicultural competence includes three components: knowledge (e.g., knowledge of multicultural therapy competencies, multicultural supervision theory), self-awareness (e.g., about gender identity, racial identity), and skills (e.g., culturally sensitive supervisory interventions) (Ancis & Ladany, 2010). Multicultural supervisor competence is essential for facilitating a successful resolution in a multicultural awareness event.

The marker of a multicultural awareness event can be obvious, as in the case when the demographics of members of the triad (client, supervisee, supervisor) are starkly different, or more subtle, such as when the multicultural differences are not visible (e.g., sexual orientation, ethnicity, ability status, family structure) or outside of awareness. The task environment consists of interaction sequences that typically include exploration of feelings, assessment of multicultural knowledge, focus on multicultural awareness, focus on skill, normalizing the experience, and focus on the supervisory alliance.

As noted previously, critical events typically do not occur in isolation. In fact, they likely overlap and connect in a myriad of ways. We now move back to the parallel process case with Arcadio and consider how a multicultural awareness event can overlap with a parallel process event.

## EXAMPLE OF A SUCCESSFULLY RESOLVED MULTICULTURAL AWARENESS EVENT

At the beginning of the foregoing case, we see that multicultural knowledge, awareness, and skill are essential in this context, inasmuch as the supervisor is a White woman, the supervisee is a Latino man who is in a wheelchair, and his clients include an able-bodied Latina woman and a White woman with a visual disability. With such differences, the supervisee's mention of gender, race, and/or disability (*or* his complete lack of attention to these!) may be the marker of a heightening multicultural awareness event.

That is, although the supervisor facilitated the working through of a parallel process event, the potential need to raise the supervisee's multicultural awareness should not be ignored. The following illustrates a multicultural awareness event that came about in Arcadio's subsequent supervision session.

Recall that the previous session ended with both supervisor and supervisee feeling fairly positive about their interaction. The supervisor continued on with her day, yet continued to reflect on the session. Although she felt that it had gone well, she could not shake her nagging feeling at its conclusion. Recognizing this feeling as potentially indicative of her own countertransference, she decided to consult with a colleague.

During this consultation, the colleague commented that there seemed to be a host of multicultural issues at play and asked whether any of these were addressed. Because the supervisor generally felt comfortable bringing up multicultural issues with her supervisees, she was surprised to realize that she had not done so in her previous session with Arcadio. Suddenly she became acutely aware of the source of her "nagging feeling." Recently, she had been diagnosed with macular degeneration, an illness of the retina that can cause blindness. No one other than her partner knew her diagnosis. She then connected her fear of going blind with Arcadio's client, Irene, who became blind following a car accident. Keeping this insight in mind, in her next supervision session with Arcadio, the supervisor began as usual:

**Supervisor:** What would you like to learn today?

**Supervisee:** Well, I'm not sure we can top last week, but I feel good about the way I was able to deal with Sylvia, my client with GAD. My other client, Irene, had to cancel our appointment because the car service that was coming to pick her up didn't show up on time. I'm really disappointed about that.

This is another choice point. The supervisor could facilitate a discussion of the parallel process with Sylvia to see how Arcadio handled the subsequent therapy session with this client. Alternatively, the supervisor could attend to Arcadio's disappointment about Irene's cancellation. Because of her insight about the failure to discuss Irene's disability during the previous supervision session, the supervisor decides to attend to the latter issue and begins by asking Arcadio to explore his disappointment.

**Supervisor:** Say more about your disappointment.

**Supervisee:** I don't know. Everything went so well with Sylvia. I was able to try out helping her stay in the here and now and she seemed to get something out of it. I was all ready to see Irene, and then I find out that she cancelled at the last minute. It feels like one step forward and one step back.

## Marker

The supervisor has little information at this point to decide whether this is the initiation of a critical event. Further exploration eventually reveals the marker of a multicultural awareness event.

**Supervisor:** Arcadio, I've seen you after clients have cancelled before, and you typically don't respond this way. What do you think might be going on? [*points out his incongruence*]

**Supervisee:** I'm not sure. It's just a big letdown, like I've let Irene down.

**Supervisor:** How so? [*notices Arcadio looking at the floor*] How are you feeling right now?

**Supervisee:** There's like a sadness and a fear all rolled into one.

**Supervisor:** Sadness and fear. [*simply repeats to encourage him to elaborate*]

**Supervisee:** Yeah, sad because I wasn't able to help her but also there's something about her that triggers a fear in me, and I don't know why.

**Supervisor:** That's interesting. Keep going with the fear and any image that comes to your mind. [*unsure whether this is Arcadio's countertransference or an indication of his lack of multicultural awareness*]

**Supervisee:** It's almost like a fear of contamination. And I keep picturing her service dog. I love dogs, but for some reason this anxiety wells up when I picture Roscoe. That's the dog's name. He's got the sweetest temperament, so there is no real reason to be afraid of him.

**Supervisor:** What does this dog represent for you, do you think? [*beginning to think that his reaction may have more to do with disability than with his feeling about the dog*]

The supervisor lets Arcadio sit with his question. It's a rather powerful question for supervision, as it is identical to what might be asked of a client.

**Arcadio:** He's a service dog. So he represents being of service to someone who is disabled. I know that's obvious, but I'm not sure where you're going with this. I'm in a wheelchair. A service dog is nice but not something I really need.

At this point the marker is clear to the supervisor. She begins to wonder about Arcadio's multicultural knowledge, particularly in relation to disability. In previous sessions they discussed Arcadio's disability, as well as disability as a multicultural identity variable. The supervisor views Arcadio as rather adept and knowledgeable about disabilities but thinks he may be limited in terms of self-awareness. Thus, she initiates the task environment of a multicultural awareness event.

## Task Environment

### Focus on Multicultural Awareness

**Supervisor:** That's true, I suppose. But perhaps we can step back for a moment. Last week when we met, you mentioned, along with feeling anxious, that you felt some fear in relation to your clients. I'm confident in your knowledge about multicultural issues, particularly in relation to disabilities. However, even when we're knowledgeable, sometimes we still have blind spots. [*this mention of "blind spots" was unintentional, however, a propos*]

**Supervisee:** How do you mean?

**Supervisor:** What kind of disability does Irene have?

**Supervisee:** She's blind, but I'm not blind. I'm in a wheelchair, which I think you can see. [*sarcastic, as he perceives her question as related to parallel process*]

**Supervisor:** Yes. Blind is not something we strive to become [*perceiving Arcadio's sarcasm as defensive, wants to facilitate his insight*]

(*pause*)

**Supervisor:** . . . any more than we strive to be in a wheelchair.

**Supervisee:** Oh God, I can't even imagine what it would be like to be blind. *And* in a wheelchair!

**Supervisor:** I suppose it'd be mighty scary.

**Arcadio:** Definitely. (*pause*). Wow. Do you think that may be where my feelings are coming from?

**Supervisor:** Perhaps. What do you suppose?

**Supervisee:** Well, it fits. I've never imagined myself becoming blind. I figured God gave me enough to deal with by putting me in this chair. That would be horrible to also be blind. I'm not sure I could take it.

**Supervisor:** So the fear makes sense and possibly distracts you from the therapy process with Irene.

**Supervisee:** You're going to find this funny, or maybe not so funny. I just realized that Irene probably doesn't know that I'm in a wheelchair. [*shows his ability to take his client's perspective, an important skill*]

**Supervisor:** Of course! Makes sense! [*delighted at his insight*]

**Supervisee:** It never really came up, and it was nice not to have someone come in and look at me in the chair for once. Instead, she was just there to be with me. But it also was probably a lost opportunity to connect with her from a disability perspective.

**Supervisor:** You're on the right track now, I think now. [*reinforces his self-awareness*]

**Supervisee:** Thank you.

**Supervisor:** So, now that you are more aware of how disability issues may be playing out with Irene, how might you handle that in your next session with her? [*wants to give him an opportunity to display his multicultural expertise*]

### Focus on the Therapeutic Process and Focus on Skill

**Supervisee:** Well, for starters we could talk about it. I could bring up my disability and how we both have physical disabilities and what that is like for Irene to know. It would give me a chance to assess her multicultural identity in relation to her disability and consider how our two identities interact. I also need to be sure not to overplay the idea that just because we both have disabilities, that our reactions have to be the same.

**Supervisor:** Go on.

**Supervisee:** Well, I have a good idea about what it's like to be in a wheelchair but really don't know what it's like to be blind.

**Supervisor:** And what about your racial difference from her?

**Supervisee:** Good point. We are different there as well, so we could discuss that . . . and also our gender differences.

**Supervisor:** So there are potentially a number of multicultural variables to go over with her. At the same time, she presents with anxiety, so that can't be forgotten. [*wants to facilitate an integrated conceptualization (i.e., diagnosis in the context of disability)*]

**Supervisee:** Of course. How do I balance it all?

**Supervisor:** Well the first thing that has to happen is that Irene needs to show up for a session!

(*Both chuckle*)

### Focus on the Supervisory Alliance

**Supervisor:** Before we go there, I want to check in with how our work has been for you so far today? [*does not want to overlook the possibility of his discomfort related to their discussion of his disability, thereby modeling cultural sensitivity*]

**Supervisee:** Well, another whirlwind of insight! I'm grateful I've had this opportunity to work in this way. I'm also embarrassed and frustrated that I didn't see the multicultural piece last week. Especially since that's all I talk about outside of supervision!

### Normalize the Experience

**Supervisor:** And like last week, I want you to know that the feelings of embarrassment and frustration are a normal reaction to recognizing things that are out of our awareness. Does that make sense?

**Supervisee:** Yes, but I hope this gets easier.

**Supervisor:** I'm not sure it ever does, but the more you do it, the quicker you'll come to the insight. Just the other day I was dealing with a clinical issue that was in my own blind spot and had to seek consultation. It's something I'm typically aware of, but not this time. The consultation helped and I was able to move on.

At this point the supervisor chose to disclose some, but not all, of her recent personal challenges and how this insight following their previous session made her realize that she had overlooked Arcadio's lack of attention to the obvious multicultural issues. A supervisor's disclosure of her own clinical struggles is powerful; it can help a supervisee reveal more of her own struggles and thereby strengthen the supervisory alliance (Ladany & Walker, 2003). Moreover, disclosure demonstrates to a supervisee how a well-timed self-disclosure in therapy can benefit a client. However, in this case the supervisor decided not to disclose the specifics of her visual impairment because she considered the information to be too personal and likely to be more in the service of the supervisor than the supervisee.

**Supervisee:** That's good to know, that with all your experience you still have to deal with things.

**Supervisor:** Well, actually, I've been struggling with whether or not to tell you this. It's personal for me, of course. I wavered between moving our conversation off of what was most important, you and the client, to a discussion about how my own personal struggle with my vision might be getting in the way of my being helpful as a supervisor to you with this case.

**Supervisee:** Jeez! I can see that. Thanks for letting me know that you, too, sometimes don't know what to do when!

**Supervisor:** Of course! In our field, the learning opportunities are never ending, which is what makes this job so exciting.

Because working on multicultural issues in supervision can be emotionally draining, it is wise to focus on the supervisory alliance to see whether supervisor and supervisee are on the same page. In addition, it is good to sum up what was learned during the session thus far and how the supervisee can generalize the supervision work to the therapy session (resolution).

### Focus on the Supervisory Alliance

**Supervisor:** But now let's get back to an important question you asked earlier. You asked how to decide when to focus on the multicultural issue and when to focus on the anxiety work. [*focuses on the task component of their alliance*]

**Supervisee:** Yes, there's so much to cover. What would you suggest?

**Supervisor:** What's it like when clients bring in multiple presenting concerns? [*empowers Arcadio to answer his own question*]

**Supervisee:** Go with where the client takes us. [*indicates knowledge of responsiveness*]

**Supervisor:** Yes, and in this case, Irene should give you an indication about where she wants to head in therapy. So far, she's made it clear that she wants to focus on her anxiety, and there are a variety of behavioral interventions to help with that. And we can certainly talk more about some of those in supervision, as well as what you've tried in the past and how it's worked. Also, you know specific multicultural interventions that you can use in your work with her.

### Resolution

**Supervisee:** That sounds good. I definitely feel good about the multicultural variables. I'd like to talk more about some of these behavioral interventions.

At this point in the supervision session, Arcadio's multicultural awareness was heightened. At the end of this event, his comment suggests a marker for a different critical event, addressing a skill difficulty (i.e., his request for assistance to help him work more effectively with his client's anxiety). At this point, the supervisor could begin another task environment, similar to the one described in Chapter 3.

However, there was an additional parallel process that occurred that was minimally broached in this last supervision event. This parallel process involved the supervisor's indecision about disclosing her impending disability to the supervisee and the supervisee's decision to keep knowledge of his disability from the client. Although the supervisor could have explained at length the fears that she was in the midst of experiencing, she determined that this disclosure would not have facilitated Arcadio's learning, and indeed she disclosed this deliberation directly. By exposing her own clinical struggle, she modeled another parallel process that facilitated Arcadio's learning, and she did so without her personal issue pulling for Arcadio's sympathy.

If the supervisor had not been aware of the multicultural issues at play, or if she had responded poorly to the multicultural issues, the multicultural event would have been unresolved. Moreover, additional diversity factors in this case illustration, namely gender and race, may prove worthy of future supervisory discourse. Thus, across and within three sessions of supervision we could witness events related to four supervision tasks: working through parallel process, heightening multicultural awareness, and remediating a skill difficulty. Addressing these tasks in event after event is like a wave that we, as supervisors, must surf, and do our best not to fall off.

## SPECIAL CONSIDERATIONS: "SUP OF SUP"

In this chapter, we primarily focused on the manner in which parallel processes occur between the therapy supervision dyad and the therapy dyad. We have also been witness to parallel processes occurring in the dyad with a supervisor and a supervisor in training, the therapy supervision dyad, and the therapy dyad. To be sure that the amount of complexity among these three dyads accelerates at each level, the same critical events approach can be used at each level and can begin at the highest level.

As a simple example, consider a client who presents with significant anxiety that does not get explored by the therapist. The therapist, in her role as supervisee, presents as uncharacteristically anxious in supervision, a behavior that is similarly overlooked by the supervisor and perhaps also experienced by the supervisor. Next, the supervisor presents to her or his supervisor (the "sup of sup") as particularly anxious. It then becomes the role of the supervision supervisor to attend to the parallel process with the therapy supervisor, who in turn, it is hoped will send it down the chain of dyads. Because there appears to be no empirical work conducted in this area, the multiple parallel processes may be a fruitful direction for future research.

## CONCLUSION

As multiple critical events become intertwined, it behooves the supervisor to parse the events to better understand the significance and focus of supervisory interventions. Managing multiple events is a supervisory skill in and of itself. In the next and final chapter, we recommend how to use our critical events in supervision model to enhance supervisory practice.

# Using the Critical Events Model in Practice and Training

In the concluding section of this book, we expand on the practice implications of the critical events in psychotherapy supervision model, first by discussing the supervision session described in this book's companion video *Critical Events in Psychotherapy Supervision*,[1] and then by considering a variety of effective and ineffective elements of supervision practice. Next, we suggest ways in which supervisors can be trained to learn about using the model. Finally, we discuss research-related approaches to how the model can be studied.

---

[1] Available for purchase at http://www.apa.org/pubs/books/4310956.aspx/.

http://dx.doi.org/10.1037/14916-006
*Supervision Essentials for the Critical Events in Psychotherapy Supervision Model,* by N. Ladany, M. L. Friedlander, and M. L. Nelson

# THE CRITICAL EVENTS IN SUPERVISION MODEL IN ACTION

For this section, we refer to the video demonstration of the critical events model. The critical event described in the companion video is working through countertransference (Ladany, Friedlander, & Nelson, 2005). In this demonstration the trainee, Tiffany, brought to supervision challenges related to a client's potential use of medical marijuana. Nicholas Ladany served as her consulting supervisor.

Tiffany identified one client in particular whose presentation was triggering reactions related to her family of origin, particularly her brother, who has a history of drug abuse, and the negative consequences that resulted from his addiction. Within the first 3 minutes of the session, Tiffany began describing her personal background and reactions in relation to this client, expressing a desire to sort how much her concerns were "personal versus clinical."

Thus, the marker in this event appeared in the initial minutes of the session. Her recognition that her concerns were of a personal nature indicated that the task for this event would be to work through countertransference. Although the construct *countertransference* originated in the psychoanalytic literature, we recognize the broader definition, applicable across theoretical approaches, reflecting the personal challenges that supervisees experience brought about by their clinical work (Ladany et al., 2005).

Once the marker was identified, the session moved into the task environment phase of the critical event. The first interactional sequence was a focus on the therapy process. That is, we began with a discussion of how the client came across to the supervisee and noted challenges attributable to the client's seeming delay in maturity (e.g., came across as at least 5 years younger than his chronological age). We then spent considerable time on the second interactional sequence, a direct focus on the supervisee's countertransference, specifically the supervisee's role in her family of origin (e.g., caretaker). The sequence exploration of feelings followed, during which the supervisee was able to tap into some intense feelings of loss and sadness, many of which stemmed from her relationship with her brother. At points we also used the sequence focus on the supervisory alliance to check in to see whether the work in which we were engaged was helping the supervisee. Tiffany indicated that she was willing to continue the work we had begun (reflecting our agreement on the tasks component of the supervisory alliance). Throughout the event, Dr. Ladany relied on empathizing with Tiffany's experience in the supervision session to strengthen the bond component of the alliance.

The final interactional sequence was attending to parallel process. The supervisor disclosed that he was having an internal conflict in the moment; that is, he was wondering if he should advise the supervisee how to proceed with her case. This happened to mirror the very question Tiffany had—should she advise the patient on whether or not it was wise to use marijuana for medicinal purposes? During this discussion of the parallel process, Tiffany was able to identify her own internal conflict about whether or not to tell the client what to do.

These interactional sequences closely match those that were identified in our original model for a working through countertransference event (Ladany et al., 2005). In the current demonstration, focusing on the supervisory working alliance was an additional interactional sequence. In this session, the alliance emerged from the figure to the ground largely because of the depth and amount of family-of-origin discussion in which Tiffany was willing to engage. In other words, Dr. Ladany continued to check in with Tiffany to ensure that the tasks of the session were mutually agreed upon and she believed she was being heard. Although Tiffany seemed willing to do so, the supervisor believed that it was important to touch base to ask her if it was acceptable for her to move to deeper levels of work. This checking in was a way in which the supervisor specifically attended to the agreement on tasks component of the supervisory working alliance.

The final phase, the resolution, occurred in the last 8 minutes of the session. During this period in the event, Dr. Ladany asked Tiffany about how the insight she seemed to gain during the supervision session might influence her therapeutic process with her client. The purpose of this discussion was to ground the supervision work in learning about therapeutic responsiveness.

Tiffany was able to identify that the primary component of the resolution was an increase in her self-awareness. She indicated a belief that this change in self-awareness would help her "be more present" with her client, and her internal struggle would be less likely to come to mind during her session: that is, it would present less of a distraction from the therapeutic process. We also explored how this new realization might help Tiffany with future clients. Although the countertransference event was "resolved" in a way that seemed productive, Tiffany acknowledged that additional work on these issues in her own personal therapy would be important for her.

In sum, the session adhered to the critical events model fairly well. Not only were the interactional sequences consistent with previous theorizing, but also the five sequences were those that Shaffer and Friedlander (2015) identified as the most relational ones in our model (exploration of feelings, focus on the therapeutic process, focus on countertransference, attend to parallel process, and focus on the supervisory alliance).

Of course, although it is advantageous that the session worked out so well, it is important to note that not all events result in a successful resolution like this one. Even with successful resolutions, the supervisor should reflect on the work and consider what might have been preferable. For example, in the session with Tiffany, upon reflection, the supervisor wondered how helpful it was to push Tiffany to consider her "worst case scenario" if her patient should decide to use marijuana. Although this focus may have helped her obtain some needed insight at that particular point, less emphasis might have saved some time for other important supervision work. Nonetheless, he hoped that, as is often the case in psychotherapy, unidentified or unfinished work in a supervision session opens the door for future meaningful work in supervision.

## EFFECTIVE AND INEFFECTIVE SUPERVISION

The practice of psychotherapy supervision is at once an art and a science, and theoretical models in supervision have only begun to capture aspects of the complexity. Theoretical models are part of the story that determines the effectiveness and ineffectiveness of supervision. Expanding on Ladany's (2013) elements of effective supervision, a variety of critical factors can be examined by scholars and reflected on by practitioners as important considerations when gauging the effectiveness of supervision.

In terms of effective supervision, the following factors should be considered:

1. *Recognize the power of the supervisory relationship.* In the critical events in supervision model, we define the relationship from the perspective of the supervisory working alliance. Over time, the strength of the supervisory relationship has demonstrated an important contribution to a variety of supervision process and outcome variables (e.g., Ladany & Inman, 2012).

2. *Use models of counseling and psychotherapy supervision.* We believe it is a mistake to depend on psychotherapy models (e.g., psychoanalytic supervision) as the sole informant or primary approach for conducting supervision. Rather, models created specifically for supervision, ones that recognize the unique processes inherent in supervision, are likely lead to better supervisory outcomes. Although we describe and illustrate the critical events in psychotherapy supervision in this book, there are other models worthy of consideration, including two from APA's Clinical Supervision Essentials Series: McNeill and Stoltenberg's (2016) integrated developmental model and Holloway's (2016) systems approach to supervision model.

3. *Recognize conditions in supervision that are unique and different from psychotherapy.* First, supervision is inherently educational. Despite its relational elements, it is a didactic endeavor in which the supervisor's primary function is to teach. Second, another primary function is evaluation, in that supervisors serve as gatekeepers for the mental health professions. Third, in most cases, supervision is an involuntary mandate for supervisees. As such, the autonomy to leave the relationship that characterizes psychotherapy does not pertain to supervision.

4. *Engage in role induction.* As noted in Chapter 2, providing supervisees with the expected roles and responsibilities at the beginning of the supervision experience can alleviate potential challenges later. Because of the potential for poor or harmful supervision experiences to occur (Ellis et al., 2014; Nelson & Friedlander, 2001), it is important not to assume that because a supervisee has received supervision previously, she knows what is expected of her.

5. *Distinguish between supervision and psychotherapy.* Although at times the processes that occur in supervision can appear identical to those that take place in therapy (e.g., exploration of feelings), supervisors should not confuse the goals of supervision (e.g., increased self-awareness to better understand a client) with the goals of psychotherapy (e.g., increased self-awareness to improve functioning).

6. *Attend to supervisee-focused and client-focused outcomes.* Sometimes it is easy for supervisors to focus on client well-being without attending sufficiently to a supervisee's learning. At times an exclusive client focus may be indicated, such as when a client is suicidal. That said, supervisors should resist the urge to attend solely to the client without regard to the supervisee.

7. *Become aware of covert processes in supervision.* Research in supervision (e.g., Mehr, Ladany, & Caskie, 2015) suggests that supervisees often keep clinically relevant material from their supervisors, possibly out of fear of negative evaluation. Nondisclosure of relevant material can clearly hinder client care as well as hamper a supervisee's learning.

8. *Develop an understanding of the ethical and legal issues pertinent to supervision.* Supervisors must contend with issues that differ from those related to therapy; such issues include vicarious liability, confidentiality, and multiple roles. It would behoove supervisors to become well-versed in the ethics and legalities of supervision without assuming that knowledge of legal and ethical issues in therapy is sufficient.

9. *Evaluate using best practices.* In part, this element of effective supervision is aspirational. To date, no best practice evaluation measures with sound psychometric properties have been developed or validated. Thus, supervisors are left with doing their professional best to ensure that the two components of evaluation (goal setting and feedback) are provided with the utmost of care.

10. *Strive for multicultural competence.* The psychology literature from the early 21st century continues to demonstrate a variety of multicultural challenges between supervisors and supervisees (e.g., microaggres-

sions) that are similar to those between therapists and clients. Thus, it behooves supervisors to remain abreast of new and emerging developments in the professional multicultural literature.

11. *Recognize the importance of parallel processes.* We discussed this element at length in Chapter 4. To reiterate, supervisors should have an understanding of how parallel processes occur and be comfortable with bringing parallel processes to their supervisees' awareness.

12. *Tend to administrative responsibilities.* Often the greatest challenge for a supervisor is to balance the "teacher" and "counselor" roles. In addition, there are a variety of administrative responsibilities to which supervisors must attend, such as note taking, supervisee monitoring, and assorted paperwork.

13. *Recognize the importance of group supervision and peer supervision.* Although our focus has been individual supervision, there is an emerging literature on how group supervision and peer supervision can serve as salient supplemental supervision activities (Avent, Wahesh, Purgason, Borders, & Mobley, 2015; Burnes, Wood, Inman, & Welikson, 2013). Supervisors should be aware that not only can the group further the learning goals of supervision but the group processes also can hinder learning, particularly when there is unacknowledged diversity within the group (cf. Friedlander et al., in press).

14. *Obtain training and supervision of supervision.* There remains a significant gap between the importance that training programs place on the development of therapy skills as compared with the development of supervisor skills. Often novice supervisors are able to develop skills only through professional development opportunities. It has yet to be determined whether these professional development activities are sufficient for developing supervisor competence. In particular, a key element is for supervisors to enhance their self-awareness in relation to their supervisory work, something that traditional professional development workshops minimally address. We encourage supervisors to seek ongoing supervision of supervision throughout their professional lives, and when supervisors discover blocks in their work, they should

enhance their ongoing supervision of supervision as well as seek therapy to better serve their supervisees and their supervisees' clients.

In contrast to effective supervisor practices, ineffective supervisor practices are important to consider as *what not to do* in supervision. In addition, it is important to recognize that the supervisees can contribute to poor supervision outcomes. We categorize these ineffective supervision elements as supervisor factors, supervisee factors, and dyadic factors.

Along with elements that reflect effective supervisory practices, there are other factors to consider. First, supervisors have been known to misapply a developmental model, resulting in supervisees feeling infantilized. In other words, some supervisors mistakenly assume that all new supervisees need a great deal of structure and feedback, without considering that many novices enter training programs with significant skills. Conversely, the assumption that advanced supervisees need little support can result in missed learning opportunities, particularly in specific areas in which a supervisee has little knowledge despite being fairly experienced and sophisticated in general conceptualization ability.

As noted, evaluation at times poses challenges to supervisors. In some ways providing critical feedback seems antithetical to the empathic and nonjudgmental approach that is the hallmark of responsive psychotherapy. Nonetheless, supervisors should be cautious about providing exceptionally positive evaluations for all supervisees because in doing so they forgo the gatekeeping role. Of course, as mentioned, supervisors often are hampered by a lack of reliable and valid instruments for evaluating supervisee competence.

Third, there are supervisors who are multiculturally misguided or bigoted in their approach to others, including supervisees, clients, staff, and members of the community. Supervisees readily pick up on their supervisors' biased beliefs and recommendations that reflect multicultural incompetence, such as sexism, racism, and homophobia (Walker et al., 2007). Given historical multicultural training differences in counseling and therapy programs, it is not unusual that supervisees come to supervision with more and better multicultural training than do their supervisors, which can result in negative supervision experiences.

Our focus has been on elements of supervisor behavior that can positively or negatively affect the work of supervision. Undoubtedly, however, supervisees also play a significant role. In terms of supervisee factors related to ineffective supervision, we have identified four factors. First, the supervisee's openness to learning and receptivity to feedback are critical for learning to occur. Second, the supervisee needs to have the capacity to learn helping skills and be trained in helping skills. Future models of therapy training may do well to spend more than one or two semesters in helping skills training. Parenthetically, helping skills are the few skills that hold promise in relation to evaluation (Hill & Lent, 2006). Third, supervisees need to have a capacity for deep self-awareness and self-reflection. To learn from supervisors, as well as from one's own experiences, supervisees need to have the ability and devote the time to understand themselves in relation to the therapeutic work. Fourth, supervisees need to have the capacity for knowledge acquisition. That said, knowledge alone (e.g., theories, research, statistics, etc.) is not sufficient for becoming a competent psychotherapist. In fact, training programs may be overemphasizing knowledge acquisition and underemphasizing skill development, which is the sine qua non of competence as a psychotherapist.

The final set of factors related to the ineffectiveness of supervision pertains to dyadic factors, of which we have identified three. As noted, a strong supervisory working alliance is a foundational aspect that contributes to the effectiveness of supervision. Similarly, a problematic alliance can be the death knell of supervision work, related to a variety of negative outcomes, including nondisclosure of relevant clinical material, dismissiveness of a supervisor's recommendations, and generally unproductive time spent in supervision. Second, supervisors who are exclusively focused on clients' outcomes are unlikely to help supervisees learn and, in fact, may lead supervisees to become resistant and unresponsive. Finally, we caution supervisors who may be inclined to have case discussions predominate in their supervision sessions. Supervision sessions that solely involve reviewing case notes, with little or no attention to the professional development goals and tasks of supervision, are inherently inadequate and potentially harmful (e.g., Friedlander, 2015).

# THE CRITICAL EVENTS IN SUPERVISION MODEL: TRAINING SUPERVISORS

The training of supervisors has gained increased attention in professional development circles over the past decade; however, specific evidence about best practices is limited. In this section we offer one method of training supervisors in applying the model. This method can be applied in two ways. First, we consider how the model can be used to review supervision work that has occurred (i.e., reflecting back), and second, we examine how to help supervisors become comfortable with the model during a supervision session and when anticipating upcoming supervision sessions (i.e., reflecting forward).

## Reflecting Back

To learn from supervisory experiences, we advocate a looking-back approach. The first step is to become familiar with the common critical events that occur in supervision (e.g., addressing skill deficits) and then reflect back on the types of critical events that have occurred in one's actual supervisory work. For example, if a skill deficit was recognized in a previous session, such as helping a supervisee learn the Gestalt two-chair technique, the supervisor could first think about the strength of the supervisory working alliance with the supervisee before and during the event. As an aid in doing so, the supervisor could use the Supervisory Working Alliance Scale (Ladany et al., 2008). Simply responding to each item may in and of itself help a supervisor consider what he should be attending to in relation to his alliance with a specific supervisee. Next, the supervisor could attempt to identify the marker that signaled the initiation of the event (e.g., the supervisee asked how to perform a Gestalt two-chair technique because he thought it may help one of his clients). Then the supervisor would consider the types of interactional sequences that occurred during that event (Table 1.1 could serve as a reference point). The interactional sequences may be identified from memory, case notes, or from a review of the recorded supervision session(s).

Once the interactional sequences have been identified, the supervisor could compare the sequences used with the ones deemed typical for each critical event in our model. Discrepancies may point to interactional sequences that could have been used (e.g., a supervisor may be reminded of normalizing the supervisee's experience). Finally, the supervisor could contemplate the extent to which that event was resolved in terms of the alliance and the supervisee's self-awareness, knowledge, and skills. For example, a supervisee may have significantly increased his knowledge of the Gestalt two-chair technique but demonstrated limited skills in applying it, indicating a partially resolved event. Moreover, a broader look at the supervision outcomes could occur (Ladany, Walker, Pate-Carolan, & Gray Evans, 2008). Based on this entire analysis, the supervisor could then consider how to assist the supervisee in subsequent supervision sessions.

### Reflecting Forward

A second approach to learning how to apply the critical events model is to anticipate various critical events and identify the necessary components. We found this approach particularly useful in supervision workshops. For example, we often show a portion of a therapy session and ask participants to assume the role of supervisor and identify the possible critical events that could occur in the next supervision session. We have them identify the potential markers, followed by the interactional sequences that are likely to be effective. Finally, we have them consider the types and range of potential event resolutions. Participants can be provided with Figure 5.1 and asked to fill in these components on the figure. Another learning option is to use the companion video, described earlier, in which the critical events model is illustrated with a live supervision case.

## RESEARCHING THE CRITICAL EVENTS IN PSYCHOTHERAPY SUPERVISION MODEL

As noted, the development of the critical events model in psychotherapy supervision was, and continues to be, empirically informed by supervision scholarship. Traditionally, task analytic approaches use two approaches toward the development and validation of models (Greenberg, 1983, 1986; Greenberg, Heatherington, & Friedlander, 1996). In one approach, the

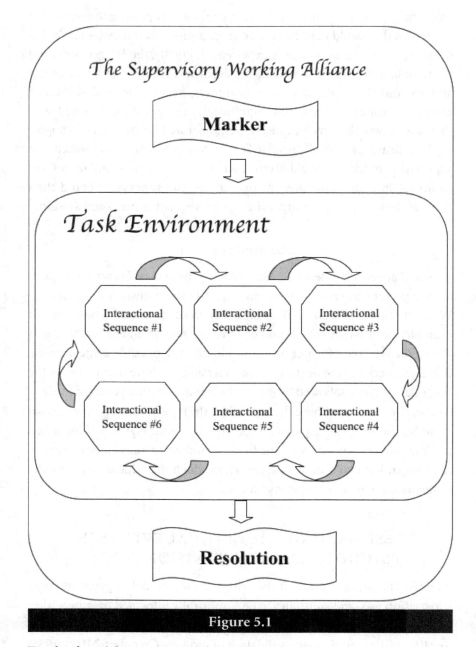

Figure 5.1

Template for training supervisors in the critical events model.

scholar identifies a recognizable task that has theoretical and empirical support. An example in the supervision literature is heightening multicultural awareness, which has garnered considerable support for its importance. Next, based on the literature, a conceptual model is created. For many of the critical events we identified and modeled, this was the approach taken.

A second approach to developing and validating the critical events model is rational–empirical in nature (Greenberg et al., 1996). In this approach, a model is derived inductively based on the intense study of a sample of successful or unsuccessful events, from which the salient interaction sequences in the task environment are identified. In our original book (Ladany et al., 2005), we suggested that researchers use a rational–empirical approach to test the various critical events using qualitative and quantitative methods. From this research, refinements of the model can occur.

A good example of how our model was tested was a study conducted by Bertsch et al. (2014), who examined gender-related critical events and their links to outcomes. Overall, these authors found that four of the interactional sequences (focus on the therapeutic process, exploration of feelings, focus on skills, and focus on self-efficacy) were related to the extent of the resolution of the event (i.e., self-awareness, skills, and the supervisory alliance but not knowledge). This study offers an important approach to testing the critical events model.

Another example in which the critical events model was tested was a study conducted by Shaffer and Friedlander (2015). In this work, the Relational Behavior Scale was developed, which measures how supervisees perceive the use of five of the 11 interactional sequences. The focus on the five interactional sequences was based on the authors' desire to examine the most relational of the interactional sequences. Initial evidence suggests that the measure is empirically supported based on their findings of a link between supervisees' perceptions of relational sequences and the supervisory alliance and evaluation of the supervisor.

We encourage future researchers to continue to explore the adequacy of the models of critical events we identified using the rational–empirical approach. For example, for the role conflict and ambiguity event in Chapter 2, we noted that exploration of feelings and focusing on the supervisory alliance were two prominent interactional sequences that could lead to a successful resolution. Using actual data of supervisory work, researchers would compare successful and unsuccessful role conflict and ambiguity events to determine the types and order of the most salient interactional sequences, as well as if they match up to the a priori model. In addition, using larger samples quantitatively could offer further evidence for the efficacy of the model. In sum, future researchers can use these approaches to determine how well our models work and discover new models for additional consideration.

## CONCLUSION

We hope that our model offers experienced supervisors and supervisors in training a heuristic model that is theoretically and empirically informed, clinically appealing, and practical. Throughout our work on this model, our intent has not changed. We encourage readers to help us refine this evolving model of supervision practice through research and clinical experiences that test the model to reach out to us for comment.

# Suggested Readings

For those interested in further developing their understanding of the critical events in psychotherapy supervision model and the supervision enterprise, we offer the following readings along with a brief description of the content of these readings.

Ekstein, R., & Wallerstein, R. S. (1958). *The teaching and learning of psychotherapy.* New York, NY: Basic Books.
   A seminal work in the supervision literature that continues to offer insights into the supervision enterprise, including concepts such as parallel process.
Ladany, N., & Friedlander, M. L. (2014). Sex and gender in professional psychology and training in professional psychology and training. In B. Johnson & N. Kaslow (Eds.), *Oxford handbook of education and training in professional psychology* (pp. 419–436). New York, NY: Oxford University Press.
   Specifically examines the role of sex and gender on supervision and training.
Ladany, N., Friedlander, M. L., & Nelson, M. L. (2005). *Critical events in psychotherapy supervision: An interpersonal approach.* Washington, DC: American Psychological Association.
   An in-depth look at the critical events in psychotherapy supervision model that illustrates a full range of critical events and expands upon the manner in which the model can be studied.

Ladany, N., Hill, C. E., Corbett, M. M., & Nutt, E. A. (1996). Nature, extent, and importance of what psychotherapy trainees do not disclose to their supervisors. *Journal of Counseling Psychology, 43*, 10–24.

An original investigation on nondisclosures in supervision that provides clinical examples of meaningful secrets that supervisees keep from their supervisors.

Ladany, N., & Inman, A. G. (2012). Training and supervision. In E. M. Altmaier, J. C. Hansen, E. M. Altmaier, & J. C. Hansen (Eds.), *The Oxford handbook of counseling psychology* (pp. 179–207). New York, NY: Oxford University Press.

A recent review of the counseling and psychotherapy supervision literature.

Ladany, N., & Walker, J. A. (2003). Supervision self-disclosure: Balancing the uncontrollable narcissist with the indomitable altruist. *Journal of Clinical Psychology, 59*, 611–621.

Offers a model for supervisor self-disclosures.

Ladany, N., Walker, J. A., Pate-Carolan, L., & Gray Evans, L. (2008). *Practicing counseling and psychotherapy: Insights from trainees, clients, and supervisors.* New York, NY: Routledge.

Provides a guidebook for practicum trainees and supervisors with process and outcome variables in supervision linked to process and outcome variables in counseling and psychotherapy.

Olk, M., & Friedlander, M. L. (1992). Role conflict and ambiguity in the supervisory experiences of counselor trainees. *Journal of Counseling Psychology, 39*, 389–397.

Offers the original conceptualization and scale validations of the constructs role conflict and ambiguity.

Bertsch, K. N., Bremer-Landau, J. D., Inman, A. G., DeBoer Kreider, E. R., Price, T. A., & DeCarlo, A. L. (2014). Evaluation of the critical events in supervision model using gender related events. *Training and Education in Professional Psychology, 8*, 174–181.

Support for the critical events model was reported in this qualitative study of supervisees, which revealed four kinds of gender-related critical events (gender discrimination, gender identity, attraction, and power dynamics) and specific interactional sequences (e.g., exploration of feelings) used by participants' supervisors during these events. Only the gender discrimination event was associated with more unfavorable supervisory alliances.

Friedlander, M. L. (2012). Therapist responsiveness: Mirrored in supervisor responsiveness. *The Clinical Supervisor, 31*, 103–119.

This article describes the intertwining of the therapeutic relationship and the supervisory relationship in terms of supervisors' responsiveness to the continually shifting needs of supervisees and their clients. Responsiveness is illustrated by the supervisor's approach to a supervisee who was highly effective with one client but who was floundering with another client.

Friedlander, M. L. (2015). Use of relational strategies to repair alliance ruptures: How responsive supervisors train responsive therapists. *Psychotherapy, 52,* 174–179.

This article uses the critical events model to discuss and illustrate supervisor responsiveness when a supervisee experiences a rupture to the therapeutic alliance with a client. The case example also illustrates how a supervisor's failure of responsiveness to the supervisee's crisis in confidence can evolve into a rupture within the supervisory alliance.

Friedlander, M. L., Blanco, S., Bernardi, S., & Shaffer, K. S. (in press). Empowering female supervisees: A feminist, multicultural and relational perspective. In M. Keitel & M. Kopala (Eds.), *Handbook of counseling women* (2nd ed.). Thousand Oaks, CA: Sage Publications.

This chapter describes and illustrates how supervisors, operating within a feminist, multicultural, and relational framework, can empower female supervisees in both individual and group supervision using interactional strategies from the critical events model. In a summary of recent literature on gender in supervision, two critical events studies on gender events are described.

Ladany, N., Friedlander, M. L., & Nelson, M. L. (2005). *Critical events in psychotherapy supervision: An interpersonal approach.* Washington, DC: American Psychological Association.

This book introduces the critical events model of supervision and uses extensive case material and dialogue to illustrate the task analytic method for resolving each of seven commonly occurring critical events: repairing gender-related misunderstandings, heightening multicultural awareness, managing sexual attraction, remediating skill difficulties and deficits, negotiating role conflicts, working through countertransference, and addressing problematic attitudes and behavior.

Nelson, M. L., & Friedlander, M. L. (2001). A close look at conflictual supervisory relationships: The trainee's perspective. *Journal of Counseling Psychology, 48*(4), 384–395. http://dx.doi.org/10.1037/0022-0167.48.4.384

The authors investigated negative supervision experiences. Among their findings, supervisees found the most negative supervisor experiences involved supervisors who were not invested in the supervisory relationship and were unwilling to work on role conflicts. Supervisees also experienced significant stress and self-doubt as a result of these experiences. Finally, supervisees found support from peers or their therapists during this difficult time.

Shaffer, K. S., & Friedlander, M. L. (in press). What do "interpersonally sensitive" supervisors do and how do supervisees experience a relational approach to supervision? *Psychotherapy Research.*

Two studies in this article introduce the Relational Behavior Scale, which assesses supervisees' perceptions of the five most relational of the 11 interactional sequences within the critical events model: exploration of feelings, focus on the therapeutic alliance, focus on countertransference, attend to parallel process, and focus on the supervisory alliance. Support for the critical events model was found in that more frequent use of these behaviors partially explained the relation between perceptions of the supervisory alliance and evaluation of the supervisor within a specific session.

Walker, J. A., Ladany, N., & Pate-Carolan, L. M. (2007). Gender-related events in psychotherapy supervision: Female trainee perspectives. *Counselling and Psychotherapy Research, 7,* 12–18.

The authors examined supportive and unsupportive gender-related events as experienced by women supervisees. The most common supportive gender-related events pertained to assistance with integrating gender in client conceptualizations and processing transference and countertransference that were gender related. The most common unsupportive gender-related events involved the supervisor stereotyping the trainee or dismissing gender-related events.

# References

Alpher, V. S. (1991). Interdependence and parallel processes: A case study of structural analysis of social behavior in supervision and short-term dynamic psychotherapy. *Psychotherapy: Theory, Research, Practice, Training, 28*, 218–231. http://dx.doi.org/10.1037/0033-3204.28.2.218

American Psychological Association. (2014). *Guidelines for clinical supervision in health service psychology.* Retrieved from http://www.apa.org/about/policy/guidelines-supervision.pdf

Ancis, J., & Ladany, N. (2010). A multicultural framework for counselor supervision: Knowledge and skills. In N. Ladany & L. Bradley (Eds.), *Counselor supervision* (4th ed., pp. 53–95). New York, NY: Routledge.

Avent, J. R., Wahesh, E., Purgason, L. L., Borders, L. D., & Mobley, A. K. (2015). A content analysis of peer feedback in triadic supervision. *Counselor Education and Supervision, 54*(1), 68–80. http://dx.doi.org/10.1002/j.1556-6978.2015.00071.x

Barnett, M. (2007). What brings you here? An exploration of the unconscious motivations of those who choose to train and work as psychotherapists and counsellors. *Psychodynamic Practice: Individuals, Groups and Organisations, 13*, 257–274. http://dx.doi.org/10.1080/14753630701455796

Bernard, J. M., & Goodyear, R. K. (2014). *Fundamentals of clinical supervision* (5th ed.). New York, NY: Pearson.

Bertsch, K. N., Bremer-Landau, J. D., Inman, A. G., DeBoer Kreider, E. R., Price, T. A., & DeCarlo, A. L. (2014). Evaluation of the critical events in supervision model using gender related events. *Training and Education in Professional Psychology, 8*, 174–181. http://dx.doi.org/10.1037/tep0000039

Blocher, D. (1983). Toward a cognitive developmental approach to counseling supervision. *The Counseling Psychologist, 11*, 27–34. http://dx.doi.org/10.1177/0011000083111006

Bordin, E. S. (1983). A working alliance based model of supervision. *The Counseling Psychologist, 11*, 35–42. http://dx.doi.org/10.1177/0011000083111007

Bromberg, P. M. (1982). The supervisory process and parallel process in psychoanalysis. *Contemporary Psychoanalysis, 18*, 92–111. http://dx.doi.org/10.1080/00107530.1982.10745678

Burnes, T. R., Wood, J. M., Inman, J. L., & Welikson, G. A. (2013). An investigation of process variables in feminist group clinical supervision. *The Counseling Psychologist, 41*(1), 86–109. http://dx.doi.org/10.1177/0011000012442653

Chen, E. C., & Bernstein, B. L. (2000). Relations of complementarity and supervisory issues to supervisory working alliance: A comparative analysis of two cases. *Journal of Counseling Psychology, 47*, 485–497. http://dx.doi.org/10.1037/0022-0167.47.4.485

Efstation, J. F., Patton, M. J., & Kardash, C. M. (1990). Measuring the working alliance in counselor supervision. *Journal of Counseling Psychology, 37*, 322–329. http://dx.doi.org/10.1037/0022-0167.37.3.322

Ekstein, R., & Wallerstein, R. S. (1958). *The teaching and learning of psychotherapy.* New York, NY: Basic Books. http://dx.doi.org/10.1037/11781-000

Ekstein, R., & Wallerstein, R. S. (1972). *The teaching and learning of psychotherapy* (Revised ed.). Oxford, UK: International Universities Press.

Ellis, M. V., Berger, L., Hanus, A. E., Ayala, E. E., Swords, B. A., & Siembor, M. (2014). Inadequate and harmful clinical supervision: Testing a revised framework and assessing occurrence. *The Counseling Psychologist, 42*, 434–472. http://dx.doi.org/10.1177/0011000013508656

Falender, C. A., & Shafranske, E. P. (2004). *Clinical supervision: A competency-based approach.* Washington, DC: American Psychological Association. http://dx.doi.org/10.1037/10806-000

Fama, L. D. (2003). *Vicarious traumatization: A concern for pre- and post-doctoral level psychology trainees?* (Unpublished doctoral dissertation). University at Albany, State University of New York.

Forrest, L., Elman, N., Gizara, S., & Vacha-Haase, T. (1999). Trainee impairment: A review of identification, remediation, dismissal, and legal issues. *The Counseling Psychologist, 27*, 627–686. http://dx.doi.org/10.1177/0011000099275001

Fouad, N. A. (2014). Competency-based education and training in professional psychology. In W. B. Johnson & N. J. Kaslow (Eds.), *The Oxford handbook of education and training in professional psychology* (pp. 105–119). New York, NY: Oxford University Press.

Friedlander, M. L. (2012). Therapist responsiveness: Mirrored in supervisor responsiveness. *The Clinical Supervisor, 31*, 103–119. http://dx.doi.org/10.1080/07325223.2012.675199

Friedlander, M. L. (2015). Use of relational strategies to repair alliance ruptures: How responsive supervisors train responsive psychotherapists. *Psychotherapy, 52*, 174–179. http://dx.doi.org/10.1037/a0037044

Friedlander, M. L., Blanco, S., Bernardi, S., & Shaffer, K. S. (in press). Empowering female supervisees: A feminist, multicultural and relational perspective. In M. Keitel & M. Kopala (Eds.), *Handbook of counseling women* (2nd ed.). Thousand Oaks, CA: Sage Publications.

Friedlander, M. L., Heatherington, L., Johnson, B., & Skowron, E. A. (1994). Sustaining engagement: A change event in family therapy. *Journal of Counseling Psychology, 41*, 438–448. http://dx.doi.org/10.1037/0022-0167.41.4.438

Friedlander, M. L., Keller, K. E., Peca-Baker, T. A., & Olk, M. E. (1986). Effects of role conflict on counselor trainees' self-statements, anxiety level, and performance. *Journal of Counseling Psychology, 33*, 73–77. http://dx.doi.org/10.1037/0022-0167.33.1.73

Friedlander, M. L., Siegel, S. M., & Brenock, K. (1989). Parallel processes in counseling and supervision: A case study. *Journal of Counseling Psychology, 36*, 149–157. http://dx.doi.org/10.1037/0022-0167.36.2.149

Friedlander, M. L., & Ward, L. G. (1984). Development and validation of the Supervisory Styles Inventory. *Journal of Counseling Psychology, 31*, 541–557. http://dx.doi.org/10.1037/0022-0167.31.4.541

Gill, S. (Ed.). (2001). *The supervisory alliance: Facilitating the psychotherapist's learning experience.* Northvale, NJ: Jason Aronson, Inc.

Grant, J., Schofield, M. J., & Crawford, S. (2012). Managing difficulties in supervision: Supervisors' perspectives. *Journal of Counseling Psychology, 59*, 528–541. http://dx.doi.org/10.1037/a0030000

Gray, L. A., Ladany, N., Walker, J. A., & Ancis, J. R. (2001). Psychotherapy trainees' experience of counterproductive events in supervision. *Journal of Counseling Psychology, 48*, 371–383. http://dx.doi.org/10.1037/0022-0167.48.4.371

Greenberg, L. S. (1983). Toward a task analysis of conflict resolution in Gestalt therapy. *Psychotherapy: Theory, Research & Practice, 20*, 190–201. http://dx.doi.org/10.1037/h0088490

Greenberg, L. S. (1986). Research strategies. In L. S. Greenberg, W. M. Pinsof, L. S. Greenberg, & W. M. Pinsof (Eds.), *The psychotherapeutic process: A research handbook* (pp. 707–734). New York, NY: Guilford Press.

Greenberg, L. S., & Foerster, F. S. (1996). Task analysis exemplified: The process of resolving unfinished business. *Journal of Consulting and Clinical Psychology, 64*, 439–446. http://dx.doi.org/10.1037/0022-006X.64.3.439

Greenberg, L. S., Heatherington, L., & Friedlander, M. L. (1996). The events-based approach to couple and family therapy research. In D. H. Sprenkle &

S. M. Moon (Eds.), *Research methods in family therapy* (pp. 411–428). New York, NY: Guilford Press.

Gross Doehrman, M. J. (1976). Parallel processes in supervision and psychotherapy. *Bulletin of the Menninger Clinic, 40*(1), 1–104.

Hill, C. E., & Lent, R. W. (2006). A narrative and meta-analytic review of helping skills training: Time to revive a dormant area of inquiry. *Psychotherapy: Theory, Research, Practice, Training, 43,* 154–172. http://dx.doi.org/10.1037/0033-3204.43.2.154

Hogan, R. A. (1964). Issues and approaches in supervision. *Psychotherapy: Theory, Research & Practice, 1,* 139–141. http://dx.doi.org/10.1037/h0088589

Holloway, E. L. (2016). *Supervision essentials for a systems approach to supervision.* Washington, DC: American Psychological Association.

Jacobsen, C. H. (2007). A qualitative single case study of parallel processes. *Counselling & Psychotherapy Research, 7,* 26–33. http://dx.doi.org/10.1080/14733140601140410

Kagan (Klein), H., & Kagan, N. I. (1997). Interpersonal process recall: Influencing human interaction. In C. J. Watkins (Ed.), *Handbook of psychotherapy supervision* (pp. 296–309). Hoboken, NJ: John Wiley & Sons, Inc.

Ladany, N. (2004). Psychotherapy supervision: What lies beneath. *Psychotherapy Research, 14,* 1–19. http://dx.doi.org/10.1093/ptr/kph001

Ladany, N. (2006). A process model for facilitating supervisee insight in supervision. In L. Castonguay & C. Hill (Eds.), *Insight in psychotherapy* (pp. 337–352). Washington, DC: American Psychological Association.

Ladany, N. (2010). Learning what not to do: Lessons from lousy educators and supervisors. In M. Trotter, J. Koch, & T. Skovholt (Eds.), *Voices from the field: Defining moments in counselor and therapist development* (pp. 98–100). New York, NY: Routledge.

Ladany, N. (2013). Conducting effective clinical supervision. In G. P. Koocher, J. C. Norcross, & B. A. Greene (Eds.), *Psychologists' desk reference* (3rd ed., pp. 727–730). New York, NY: Oxford University Press. http://dx.doi.org/10.1093/med:psych/9780199845491.003.0140

Ladany, N., Brittan-Powell, C. S., & Pannu, R. K. (1997). The influence of supervisory racial identity interaction and racial matching on the supervisory working alliance and supervisee multicultural competence. *Counselor Education and Supervision, 36,* 284–304. http://dx.doi.org/10.1002/j.1556-6978.1997.tb00396.x

Ladany, N., Ellis, M. V., & Friedlander, M. L. (1999). The supervisory working alliance, trainee self-efficacy, and satisfaction. *Journal of Counseling & Development, 77,* 447–455. http://dx.doi.org/10.1002/j.1556-6676.1999.tb02472.x

Ladany, N., & Friedlander, M. L. (1995). The relationship between the supervisory working alliance and trainees' experience of role conflict and role ambiguity. *Counselor Education and Supervision, 34*, 220–231. http://dx.doi.org/10.1002/j.1556-6978.1995.tb00244.x

Ladany, N., & Friedlander, M. L. (2014). Sex and gender in professional psychology and training in professional psychology and training. In B. Johnson & N. Kaslow (Eds.), *Oxford handbook of education and training in professional psychology* (pp. 419–436). New York, NY: Oxford University Press.

Ladany, N., Friedlander, M. L., & Nelson, M. L. (2005). *Critical events in psychotherapy supervision: An interpersonal approach.* Washington, DC: American Psychological Association. http://dx.doi.org/10.1037/10958-000

Ladany, N., Hill, C. E., Corbett, M. M., & Nutt, E. A. (1996). Nature, extent, and importance of what psychotherapy trainees do not disclose to their supervisors. *Journal of Counseling Psychology, 43*, 10–24. http://dx.doi.org/10.1037/0022-0167.43.1.10

Ladany, N., & Inman, A. G. (2012). Training and supervision. In E. M. Altmaier & J. C. Hansen (Eds.), *The Oxford handbook of counseling psychology* (pp. 179–207). New York, NY: Oxford University Press.

Ladany, N., Inman, A. G., Hill, C. E., Knox, S., Crook-Lyon, R. E., Thompson, B. J., . . . Walker, J. A. (2012). Corrective relational experiences in supervision. In L. G. Castonguay & C. E. Hill (Eds.), *Transformation in psychotherapy: Corrective experiences across cognitive behavioral, humanistic, and psychodynamic approaches* (pp. 335–352). Washington, DC: American Psychological Association. http://dx.doi.org/10.1037/13747-016

Ladany, N., Lehrman-Waterman, D., Molinaro, M., & Wolgast, B. (1999). Psychotherapy supervisor ethical practices: Adherence to guidelines, the supervisory working alliance, and supervisee satisfaction. *The Counseling Psychologist, 27*, 443–475. http://dx.doi.org/10.1177/0011000099273008

Ladany, N., O'Brien, K., Hill, C. E., Melincoff, D. S., Knox, S., & Petersen, D. (1997). Sexual attraction toward clients, use of supervision, and prior training: A qualitative study of predoctoral psychology interns. *Journal of Counseling Psychology, 44*, 413–424. http://dx.doi.org/10.1037/0022-0167.44.4.413

Ladany, N., & O'Shaughnessy, T. (2015). Training and supervision in career counseling. In P. J. Hartung, M. L. Savickas, & W. B. Walsh (Eds.), *APA handbook of career intervention, Volume 1: Foundations* (pp. 375–387). Washington, DC: American Psychological Association. http://dx.doi.org/10.1037/14438-020

Ladany, N., & Walker, J. A. (2003). Supervisor self-disclosure: Balancing the uncontrollable narcissist with the indomitable altruist. *Journal of Clinical Psychology, 59*, 611–621. http://dx.doi.org/10.1002/jclp.10164

Ladany, N., Walker, J., & Melincoff, D. S. (2001). Supervisor style, the supervisory working alliance, and supervisor self-disclosures. *Counselor Education and Supervision, 40,* 263–275. http://dx.doi.org/10.1002/j.1556-6978.2001.tb01259.x

Ladany, N., Walker, J. A., Pate-Carolan, L., & Gray Evans, L. (2008). *Practicing counseling and psychotherapy: Insights from trainees, clients, and supervisors.* New York, NY: Routledge.

Lehrman-Waterman, D. E., & Ladany, N. (2001). Development and validation of the Evaluation Process within Supervision Inventory. *Journal of Counseling Psychology, 48,* 168–177.

Mallinckrodt, B., & Nelson, M. L. (1991). Counselor training level and the formation of the psychotherapeutic working alliance. *Journal of Counseling Psychology, 38,* 133–138. http://dx.doi.org/10.1037/0022-0167.38.2.133

McNeill, B. W., & Stoltenberg, C. D. (2016). *Supervision essentials for the integrative developmental model.* Washington, DC: American Psychological Association.

Mehr, K. E., Ladany, N., & Caskie, G. L. (2015). Factors influencing trainee willingness to disclose in supervision. *Training and Education in Professional Psychology, 9,* 44–51. http://dx.doi.org/10.1037/tep0000028

Melincoff, D. S. (2001). Counselor trainees' sexual attraction toward their supervisors: A qualitative study. *Dissertation Abstracts International, 62*(4-B), 2069.

Melincoff, D. S., Walker, J. A., Tyson, A., Muse-Burke, J. L., & Ladany, N. (2001, August). *Sexual attraction to supervisors: Understanding trainee experiences.* Paper presented at the meeting of the Society for Psychotherapy Research, Montevideo, Uruguay.

Mothersole, G. (1999). Parallel process. *The Clinical Supervisor, 18,* 107–121. http://dx.doi.org/10.1300/J001v18n02_08

Mueller, W. J., & Kell, B. L. (1972). *Coping with conflict: Supervising counselors and psychotherapists.* East Norwalk, CT: Appleton-Century-Crofts.

Nelson, M. L., Barnes, K. L., Evans, A. L., & Triggiano, P. J. (2008). Working with conflict in clinical supervision: Wise supervisors' perspectives. *Journal of Counseling Psychology, 55,* 172–184. http://dx.doi.org/10.1037/0022-0167.55.2.172

Nelson, M. L., & Friedlander, M. L. (2001). A close look at conflictual supervisory relationships: The trainee's perspective. *Journal of Counseling Psychology, 48,* 384–395.

Nelson, M. L., Gray, L. A., Friedlander, M. L., Ladany, N., & Walker, J. A. (2001). Toward relationship-centered supervision: A reply to Veach (2001) & Ellis (2001). *Journal of Counseling Psychology, 48,* 407–409. http://dx.doi.org/10.1037/0022-0167.48.4.407

Olk, M., & Friedlander, M. L. (1992). Trainees' experiences of role conflict and role ambiguity in supervisory relationships. *Journal of Counseling Psychology, 39,* 389–397. http://dx.doi.org/10.1037/0022-0167.39.3.389

Rabinowitz, F. E., Heppner, P. P., & Roehlke, H. J. (1986). Descriptive study of process and outcome variables of supervision over time. *Journal of Counseling Psychology, 33,* 292–300. http://dx.doi.org/10.1037/0022-0167.33.3.292

Raichelson, S. H., Herron, W. G., Primavera, L. H., & Ramirez, S. M. (1997). Incidence and effects of parallel process in psychotherapy supervision. *The Clinical Supervisor, 15,* 37–48. http://dx.doi.org/10.1300/J001v15n02_03

Ramos-Sánchez, L., Esnil, E., Goodwin, A., Riggs, S., Touster, L. O., Wright, L. K., . . . Rodolfa, E. (2002). Negative supervisory events: Effects on supervision and supervisory alliance. *Professional Psychology: Research and Practice, 33,* 197–202.

Rhodes, R. H., Hill, C. E., Thompson, B. J., & Elliott, R. (1994). Client retrospective recall of resolved and unresolved misunderstanding events. *Journal of Counseling Psychology, 41,* 473–483. http://dx.doi.org/10.1037/0022-0167.41.4.473

Rice, L. N., & Saperia, E. P. (1984). Task analysis of the resolution of problematic reactions. In L. N. Rice & L. S. Greenberg (Eds.), *Patterns of change: Intensive analysis of psychotherapy process* (pp. 29–66). New York, NY: Guilford Press.

Riggs, S. A., & Bretz, K. M. (2006). Attachment processes in the supervisory relationship: An exploratory investigation. *Professional Psychology: Research and Practice, 37,* 558–566. http://dx.doi.org/10.1037/0735-7028.37.5.558

Rogers, C. (1951). *Client-centered therapy: Its current practice, implications and theory.* London, UK: Constable.

Safran, J. D., & Muran, J. C. (1996). The resolution of ruptures in the therapeutic alliance. *Journal of Consulting and Clinical Psychology, 64,* 447–458. http://dx.doi.org/10.1037/0022-006X.64.3.447

Sarnat, J. E. (2016). *Supervision essentials for psychodynamic psychotherapies.* Washington, DC: American Psychological Association. http://dx.doi.org/10.1037/14802-000

Searles, H. F. (1955). The informational value of the supervisor's emotional experiences. *Psychiatry, 18,* 135–146.

Shaffer, K. S., & Friedlander, M. L. (2015). What do "interpersonally sensitive" supervisors do and how do supervisees experience a relational approach to supervision? *Psychotherapy Research, 14,* 1–12.

Skovholt, T. M., & Ronnestad, M. H. (1992). Themes in therapist and counselor development. *Journal of Counseling and Development, 70,* 505–515.

Sripada, B. (1999). A comparison of a failed supervision and a successful supervision of the same psychoanalytic case. *The Annual of Psychoanalysis, 26–27,* 219–241.

Strong, S. R., & Matross, R. P. (1973). Change processes in counseling and psycho-therapy. *Journal of Counseling Psychology, 20*, 25–37. http://dx.doi.org/10.1037/h0034055

Tracey, T. J., Bludworth, J., & Glidden-Tracey, C. E. (2012). Are there parallel processes in psychotherapy supervision? An empirical examination. *Psychotherapy, 49*, 330–343. http://dx.doi.org/10.1037/a0026246

Walker, J. A. (2003). *Countertransference in therapy and supervision: Proximal parallel process* (Unpublished doctoral dissertation). Lehigh University, Bethlehem, PA.

Walker, J. A., Ladany, N., & Pate-Carolan, L. M. (2007). Gender-related events in psychotherapy supervision: Female trainee perspectives. *Counselling & Psychotherapy Research, 7*, 12–18. http://dx.doi.org/10.1080/14733140601140881

Ward, L. G., Friedlander, M. L., Schoen, L. G., & Klein, J. G. (1985). Strategic self-presentation in supervision. *Journal of Counseling Psychology, 32*, 111–118. http://dx.doi.org/10.1037/0022-0167.32.1.111

# Index

# About the Authors

**Nicholas Ladany, PhD,** is the dean of the School of Leadership and Education Sciences at the University of San Diego. He previously served as dean of the School of Education and Counseling Psychology at Santa Clara University in Santa Clara, California; director of the Counseling Program at Loyola Marymount University in Los Angeles, California; chair of the Department of Education and Human Services and program coordinator and director of doctoral training of the Counseling Psychology Program at Lehigh University in Bethlehem, Pennsylvania; and has served as a faculty member at Temple University and the University of Maryland, College Park. He received his doctorate from the University at Albany, State University of New York, in 1992. Dr. Ladany has more than 80 publications and has conducted more than 240 national and international presentations in more than 20 countries in the area of counseling and psychotherapy supervision and training. In particular, his primary research interest and activity include such issues as the working alliance, self-disclosures and nondisclosures, multicultural training, ethics, and social justice. He has served as an associate editor of *Psychotherapy: Theory, Research, Practice, and Training* and as a member of the editorial boards of the *Journal of Counseling Psychology, The Counseling Psychologist,* and *Counselor Education and Supervision.* He has published five books, including *Practicing Counseling and Psychotherapy: Insights From Trainees, Clients, and Supervisors; Critical Events in Psychotherapy Supervision: An Interpersonal Approach;* and *Counselor Supervision* (4th ed.).

**Myrna L. Friedlander, PhD,** is a professor in the Counseling Psychology PhD program at the University at Albany, State University of New York, where she served as training director from 1999 to 2016. She has supervised master's and doctoral students for more than 35 years and published more than 140 book chapters and journal articles, including several self-report instruments and observational coding systems, primarily related to the processes of psychotherapy and supervision. In 2006 she coauthored *Therapeutic Alliances With Couples and Families: An Empirically Informed Guide to Practice.* A fellow of the American Psychological Association, Dr. Friedlander has served on the editorial boards of six journals and received awards for her lifetime contribution to research by the University at Albany, the Society for Counseling Psychology (American Psychological Association), and the American Family Therapy Association. A licensed psychologist in New York State, she has been in independent practice for more than 30 years.

**Mary Lee Nelson, PhD,** is retired and serving as an adjunct professor at the University of Missouri–St. Louis, where she teaches supervision theory, research, and practice. She previously was visiting professor of counseling and family therapy at the University of Missouri–St. Louis; professor and department chair of counseling psychology at the University of Wisconsin–Madison; and associate professor of counseling in educational psychology at the University of Washington. Dr. Nelson also served as staff psychologist in student counseling services at the University of Oregon, University of Washington, and University of Missouri–St. Louis and maintained a private practice in Seattle, Washington. She currently is a licensed psychologist in the state of Missouri. Dr. Nelson conducted research and published articles on interpersonal process in supervision for more than 20 years. She has served on the editorial boards of *The Counseling Psychologist, Psychotherapy Research, The Clinical Supervisor,* and the *Journal of Counseling and Development.*